Creative Lettering

Creative Lettering

TECHNIQUES & TIPS FROM TOP ARTISTS

JENNY DOH

LARK

LARK

An Imprint of Sterling Publishing
387 Park Avenue South
New York, NY 10016

ISBN 978-1-4547-0400-3

Library of Congress Cataloging-in-Publication Data

Doh, Jenny.
  Creative lettering : techniques & tips from top artists / Jenny Doh.
    pages cm
  Includes index.
  ISBN 978-1-4547-0400-3
  1. Lettering--Technique. I. Title.
  NK3600.D64 2013
  745.6'1--dc23
                                2012021130

Distributed in Canada by Sterling Publishing
c/o Canadian Manda Group, 165 Dufferin Street
Toronto, Ontario, Canada M6K 3H6
Distributed in the United Kingdom by GMC Distribution Services
Castle Place, 166 High Street, Lewes, East Sussex, England BN7 1XU
Distributed in Australia by Capricorn Link (Australia) Pty. Ltd.
P.O. Box 704, Windsor, NSW 2756, Australia

For information about custom editions, special sales, and premium
and corporate purchases, please contact Sterling Special Sales at
800-805-5489 or specialsales@sterlingpublishing.com.

Email academic@larkbooks.com for information about desk and
examination copies. The complete policy can be found at larkcrafts.com.

Every effort has been made to ensure that all the information in
this book is accurate. However, due to differing conditions, tools,
and individual skills, the publisher cannot be responsible for
any injuries, losses, and other damages that may result from
the use of the information in this book.

Some of the terms included in the book may be trademarks or
registered trademarks. Use of such terms does not imply any
association with or endorsement by such trademark owners and no
association or endorsement is intended or should be inferred. This
book is not authorized by, and neither the Author nor the Publisher is
affiliated with the owners of the trademarks referred to in the book.

Manufactured in China

2 4 6 8 10 9 7 5 3

larkcrafts.com

Editor Jenny Doh

Copyeditors Nancy D. Wood,
Amanda Crabtree Weston

Assistant Editors Jennifer Taylor,
Kerri Winterstein, Monica Mouet,
Jana Holstein

Designer Raquel Joya

Photographer Cynthia Shaffer

Table of Contents

INTRODUCTION.................................6

BASICS 7

Flora Chang 10

Jessica Swift 20

Pam Garrison.................................28

François Bégnez 36

Karyn Denten 46

Aimee Dolich.................................52

Andy Ainger.................................58

Linda Schneider 68

Lori Vliegen.................................74

Madeline Tompkins 82

Stine Kaasa 90

Lisa Engelbrecht.................................100

Philippe Debongnie 108

Barbara Close.................................118

Rhianna Wurman 126

Martha Lever 134

ABOUT THE CONTRIBUTORS.................................142

INDEX/ABOUT THE AUTHOR.................................144

Introduction

Welcome to *Creative Lettering*! Hand lettering has risen in popularity over the last few years, and it's no secret as to why—it adds panache, and anybody can do it. If you know how to write the alphabet, all you need is a little practice to gain lettering as a useful and beautiful new skill set.

Lettering can elevate any handwritten task, from addressing and penning letters to writing names on gift tags and place cards. Including even one hand-lettered word in a mixed-media piece adds meaning, and lettering adds personality to any creative memory craft or journaling page.

So grab your pen and paper, and prepare to be blown away by all you can do with hand lettering. On behalf of all the artists featured in this book and the team that worked so hard to put it together, I am honored that you have joined us, as we discover together the joy, beauty, and art of creative lettering.

Jenny Doh

places TO find ISPIRATION for LETTERING words by hANds

Basics

Hand lettering has many terms in common with computer-generated typography, such as ascender, descender, and baseline, but it also has a vocabulary of its own. A complete computer-generated alphabet is called a font, while a hand-lettered alphabet is referred to as a style or hand. Technology has borrowed freely from calligraphy, producing a number of script fonts that mimic hand lettering.

Other terms that describe letters or lettering are:

Bold is a font weight in which the letters are darker and thicker than the standard weight of surrounding letters. Bold treatment makes certain words stand out, and is often used for titles or headlines.

Italic letters slant slightly to the right.

Chunky is a term used by modern lettering artists to refer to letters that are short, thick, and "overweight."

Cursive letters are written in a flowing style and joined together.

Downstrokes are formed by moving a pen from the top of a letter to the bottom. A calligrapher typically uses more pressure to make the downstroke thicker than other parts of the letter.

Leading is the amount of space between lines of words, usually measured from the base of a word to the base of the word below it (baseline to baseline).

ANATOMY OF A LETTER

Within the world of hand lettering, there are terms for the various parts of letters, as well as the spaces on the paper where the letters get created. For example:

The **cap line** (1) is the line above the mean line, where the upper portion of capital letters reach.

The **mean line** (2), also known as the "midline," is halfway between the baseline and the cap line.

The **baseline** (3), also known as the "writing line," is where the bottom portion of the letter rests, with the exception of the descender.

The **ascender** (4) is the portion of a lowercase letter that extends beyond the mean line.

The **descender** (5) is the portion of a letter that extends below the baseline.

Lowercase refers to non-capital letters.

Monoline is a style of lettering that does not have the usual thick and thin variations of regular calligraphy. The pen used for this style is not chisel-tipped.

Uppercase is another word for capital letters.

Upstrokes are made with a pen from the bottom of a letter to the top. A calligrapher typically uses less pressure to make that portion of the letter thin.

Featured Fonts and Styles/Hands

As you read this book, you will find that each contributor has developed one or more complete alphabets in his or her own unique hand. These alphabets are provided for you to study and to be inspired by, as you delve into the wonders of creative lettering. The artists have also provided instructions for fun and unique lettering projects that utilize some of their favorite signature methods. Many of the projects and alphabets are new inventions, while others are based on traditional fonts and hands. Some of these are as follows (see Serif and Sans Serif Defined on page 49).

Futura is a typeface developed in 1927, based on geometric sans serif shapes.

Gothic is an outdated term that refers to sans serif typeface.

Helvetica is a universally recognized and very popular typeface developed in 1957, based on sans serif shapes.

Times New Roman is a serif typeface developed in 1931, commonly used in many newspapers.

Copperplate Script, also known as "English roundhand," is a calligraphy style made with a pointed pen, with downstrokes creating thick letter portions and upstrokes creating thin letter portions.

Roundhand, also known as "Foundational," is a style of hand lettering similar to Copperplate Script, with a more subtle contrast between the thick and thin strokes.

HOT-PRESSED, COLD-PRESSED, AND ROUGH PAPER

To make cold-pressed watercolor paper, the paper material is fed through cold cylinders; this results in paper that is slightly textured and therefore rough to the touch. To make hot-pressed watercolor paper, the paper material is fed through hot cylinders, resulting in paper that is smooth to the touch. Rough paper is a rougher version of cold-pressed paper.

Versals is a lettering style used in medieval works, typically to create extremely ornate initial characters on a page or chapter.

Spencerian Script is a formal calligraphic lettering style developed in 1840 that is similar to cursive writing.

Uncial is a lettering style that uses only capital letters. Generally, the first letter of sentences and documents are made larger, with ornamentation, to distinguish them from the other letters.

Materials and Supplies

A wide variety of writing tools and materials are used by the artists in this book. Here are some general terms to acquaint you with them.

ACRYLIC PAINT Fast-drying water-based paint, with results that can resemble a watercolor or oil painting; the paint, when dry, is opaque.

CD MARKER Soft-tipped marker with quick-drying ink, designed not to smear on CD/DVD surfaces.

CHISEL-TIP MARKER A style of felt-tipped marker that has an angled point, with a marking capability that resembles a calligraphy pen.

COLLAGE An art form in which a variety of papers, fabric, photos, and/or other relatively flat items are arranged and glued on paper.

CRAFT KNIFE This metal knife, also called a utility knife, has a razor-sharp blade that can be replaced when dull. When using a craft knife to cut paper, use a metal ruler and be very careful where you put your fingers.

DIP PEN This type of pen, which usually comes with a variety of nibs, is literally dipped into a bottle of ink; it does not come with an internal ink cartridge.

FRISKET Masking liquid that can be applied to paper to protect and prevent the masked portion from absorbing color or marks from other liquids and materials. The dried frisket remains tacky and can be removed from the paper.

GEL PEN A pen with water-based ink that tends to be thick and opaque, resulting in rich pigments on the page.

GESSO This white paint mixture is used to prepare/prime surfaces for painting. In journaling, gesso can be used to paint over colored surfaces for a muting or mottling effect.

GOUACHE A form of watercolor paint that is opaque rather than transparent.

GUM ARABIC A liquid binding agent derived from the hardened sap of acacia trees. It is used by calligraphers to mix with inks and watercolors to control its viscosity.

INK Ink comes in many colors, forms, and thicknesses. It can be permanent or water-soluble, and can be applied with an airbrush, pen, or a brush. Ink sprays are also available.

LIGHT BOX Contains a backlit piece of glass or Plexiglass; used by artists for tracing.

NIB The tip of a pen, the part that releases ink onto a page. Many types, sizes, and shapes are available.

POINTED PEN Calligraphy pens consist of a pen holder (the part that is held in the hand) and a nib. A pointed pen refers to a pen holder with a sharp, pointed nib, rather than a broad-edge nib. Pointed pens can produce thick and thin lines, based on the amount of pressure placed on the nib by the calligrapher.

QUILL PEN An early writing implement with a nib made from the feather of a large bird.

RUBBER CEMENT PICKUP A small square piece of soft but firm rubber that can be used like an eraser to remove excess masking fluid, rubber cement, or liquid frisket.

WALNUT INK Literally, ink made from the husk of a walnut. Often used to stain and darken paper to make it look older.

WATERCOLOR PAINT Paint made with pigments suspended in a water-soluble medium; when dry, the colors are transparent.

WORKABLE FIXATIVE Spray liquid sealer that provides a layer of protection for artwork, including pencils, pens, watercolors, and inks.

MIRACLES IN RETELLING IN SMALL LETTERS OF THE SAME STORY WHICH IS WRITTEN ACROSS THE WHOLE WORLD LETTERS TOO LARGE SOME OF US

Flora Chang

www.happydoodleland.blogspot.com

I am first a doodler and then a lettering artist. I really didn't do much lettering until I started working as a greeting card designer. I integrate illustration with lettering for most of my works, and I treat lettering as part of the illustration. My lettering style is casual, whimsical, and organic. When I illustrate, I love shapes and lines that are not perfect, and that shows in my lettering, too.

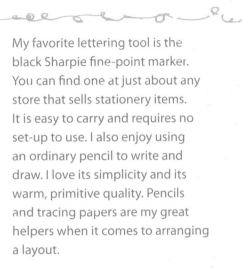

FAVORITE WRITING INSTRUMENTS

My favorite lettering tool is the black Sharpie fine-point marker. You can find one at just about any store that sells stationery items. It is easy to carry and requires no set-up to use. I also enjoy using an ordinary pencil to write and draw. I love its simplicity and its warm, primitive quality. Pencils and tracing papers are my great helpers when it comes to arranging a layout.

FAVORITE LETTER

I've always favored the letter "R." I just love the shape, plus it sounds funny.

Doodle Words

I made this piece with a hope that it would appeal to kids. It was a lot of fun to do and I think it's a lot of fun to look at. The key to this method is to just have fun as you letter and draw, without too much planning. Do not make any practice sketch. Just start lettering and doodling and try to fill up the whole page with words and symbols. Before you know it, your entire page will come to life.

fig. A

fig. B

fig. C

WHAT YOU'LL NEED

* Hot-pressed watercolor paper
* Black fine-point permanent marker
* Red dual-tip permanent marker

TECHNIQUE

The steps shown here are for just one section, where I lettered the word "lucky."

1 Doodle an oval shape with scallops, using a black permanent fine-point marker.

2 Create chunky letters to spell "Lucky." Allow the size and shape of each letter to be a little bit wonky and non-uniform (**fig. A**).

3 Create assorted dots, lines, mitered edge triangles, and scallops to decorate the letters' spaces (**fig. B**).

4 Add color to the letters and the oval, using both the broad and fine tips of the dual-tip red permanent marker. Use the broad tip to color the large areas and the fine tip to add details (**fig. C**).

5 Use similar methods with slight variances to create more words and doodles until the entire page is filled.

FAN OF SIMPLICITY

I am a big fan of simplicity; most of my artworks contain a limited color palette. But at the same time, I am also crazy about unexpected color combinations and a page full of doodles and lettering. It depends on what kind of emotion you want to convey and who your audience is. Either way, it needs to be visually appealing.

I used four colors for this piece, but once you understand the approach, you can decide to use more than just four. First, use a pencil and a ruler to draw out equally spaced horizontal guidelines on watercolor paper. Very lightly sketch in the letters with a pencil, making sure that the top and bottom of all letters touch the guidelines. Use a dip pen or a permanent marker to trace over the letters and let dry. Add washes of watercolors to the spaces between the letters and lines and let dry. Erase the pencil guidelines.

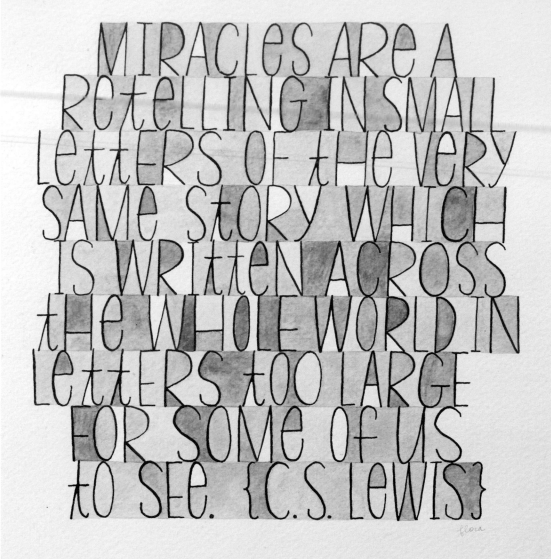

BY HAND AND BY COMPUTER

Hand-constructed letters have a charming warm quality that cannot be duplicated by a computer. However, a computer can bring your lettering to another level and achieve effects that can't be done by hand. Both methods are great, and I combine them in my works. I'll start lettering by hand, scan it into the computer, and then either trace over it or retouch it and add textures, shadows, and so on.

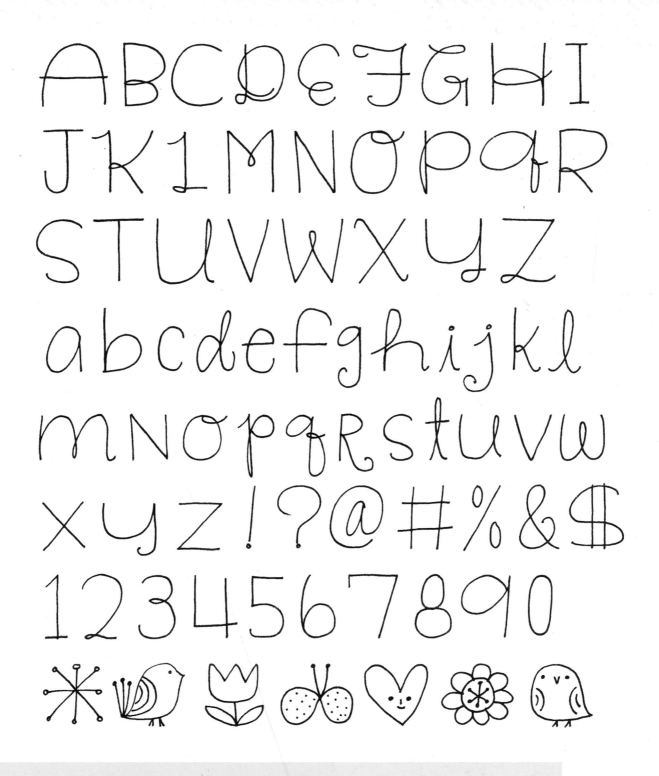

This fresh and fun alphabet celebrates the joy of doodling and simplicity. The uppercase and lowercase letters were created with strokes with even and consistent pressure, allowing the lines to have no thick or thin parts. The small doodles were drawn in the same manner, to complement the letters and numbers.

The first step to making letters with a scratchboard is to trim a piece of paper the same size as the scratchboard. Sketch the letters on the paper. Lay the paper on top of the scratchboard and lightly trace over the sketch, using a pencil. Doing this will leave light markings on the scratchboard. Use a scratchboard tool to scrape away the negative space surrounding the light markings. Color the scratched areas using scratchboard inks. One lesson I learned is to always scratch with a top to bottom motion. Rotate the board as often as you want when you scratch, but always scratch from top to bottom to make sure the lines flow smoothly.

Letter and doodle all over the blank ornament with a black pencil from a colored-pencil set. These colored pencils have a waxy texture and are less likely to smudge when you accidentally touch the lines. But still, be careful where you lay your fingers as you rotate the ornament when you draw. If you are worried about smudging, you can always spray some workable fixative as you go. When you are done, spray layers of matte varnish to protect the ornament. This one is a Christmas ornament, but you can create an ornament for any occasion with different words.

happy plate

The most important tip for this piece is to not erase any lines, even if you don't like what you've just drawn, because it will make a huge smudging disaster. Just keep on going and draw until you fill up the whole space. It's a project that should be fun and not perfect.

1. Wipe a wooden plate clean, then spray paint the top side of the plate with a color of your choice. It may need a couple of coats for full coverage. Make sure the paint dries in between coats.

2. Sand away the paint along the edge of the plate with fine-grit sandpaper. You can gently sand the painted surface too, if your paint looks too glossy.

3. Letter and doodle all over the painted surface using an 8B black graphite pencil. Be very careful where you hold the plate, because the graphite pencil lines smudge easily.

4. When done, spray matte varnish over the entire plate to protect it. This plate is not intended for food. It's for decoration only.

r

For this piece, I used a pencil to lightly sketch the outline of the letter. I used a black fine-point permanent marker to doodle within the sketched outline. It's important to make sure the doodles do not go past the sketched outline while at the same time making sure that they go all the way to them. This way, when the outline is erased, the doodles form the intended letter nicely.

Jessica Swift

www.jessicaswift.com

Starting when I was about 9 years old, for every holiday or birthday that rolled around, I created a giant bubble-letter poster—and my family came to expect it! Each hand-drawn letter was filled in with a hand-drawn pattern, and the posters were wild and colorful. That's definitely when I became hooked. I had every variety of colored marker that existed, and I used them pretty much daily. Color and pattern have always been my thing!

FAVORITE LETTER

My favorite letter is "E," I think. I love how it looks all by itself. It's fun to draw, and it seems complete somehow. Sometimes I wish my name started with an "E" because I love how it looks when people end emails with just that first letter of their name. It looks so cute!

FAVORITE WRITING INSTRUMENTS

I really love a good felt-tip marker. My favorites lately are the Tombow Dual Brush Pens. The ink is just lovely, and they're double-sided! Each end has a different tip, one for more contouring and one for straight, uniform lines. I also love simple black Pilot Precise V5 rolling ball pens (nothing too fancy). You can get both at pretty much any art supply store. I can also never resist colorful markers. I like being able to draw smooth, straight lines, and these help me achieve that.

You Are Magnificent

Purple is not a color that I use very often, so it was a fun experiment pairing it with orange. I used a somewhat restrained palette with those two colors and a few others. I drew the words first, then embellished the words, then I started doodling around the outsides. I added more detail until the piece felt finished.

fig. A

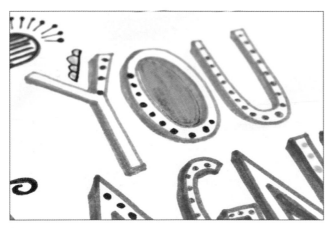

fig. B

jessica swift 23

WHAT YOU'LL NEED

* Colored markers
* Heavyweight paper

TECHNIQUE

1 Create tall and thin block letters using a colored marker (**fig. A**).

2 Create shading by adding thickness to the left and lower portions of the letters with the same colored marker (**fig. A**).

3 Add dots of color within the body of the letters. Add blocks of color to letters that have an enclosed section, such as the "e" and the "o" (**fig. A**).

4 With assorted colors, add flourishes and doodles in an intuitive, freeform manner to fill the rest of the page (**fig. B**).

CREATING FONTS AND HANDS

I'm not very technically savvy and therefore don't know how to make real fonts digitally. I just like drawing words, whether it is by hand on paper or by hand on a Wacom tablet. I admire people who create fonts digitally, and I'm glad they're out there creating beautiful fonts for me to use in my work! I think both ways of lettering are great for different reasons, and in different contexts and types of work.

Jessica's ABCs

I normally work digitally, by drawing in black ink and then scanning the letters into my computer. I then use Photoshop or Illustrator to add color. For this piece, though, I used markers. The curve ball was that I didn't have a large enough selection of colors, so the colors are not as vibrant as I wanted. The color combinations are not necessarily what I would use if I were coloring digitally. But I rolled with it, and I think it's whimsical and shows a variety of ways to create hand-drawn letters. It reminded me of my days as a kid, drawing bubble-letter posters and filling them in with patterns!

WHAT YOU'LL NEED

* Colored markers
* Heavyweight paper

TECHNIQUE

(See **fig. A**.)

The Letter D

1 Draw a block letter, but add a small flourish in the middle section on both the left and right sections.

2 Draw a line in the center of the lines that create the block letter.

3 Color the upper/outer portion and the lower/inner section of the letter red.

4 Color the remaining sections orange.

5 Outline the letter in yellow.

The Letter R

1 Draw a thin block letter without any flourishes.

2 Color the upper portion of the letter gray and the lower section red.

3 Outline the letter in pink.

4 Outline again in brown and add small dots of red at the corners on top of the pink.

The Letter F

1 Create a chunky block letter. Draw a series of small quarter-circles in the top left corner, then add diagonal lines that spread from there out into the rest of the letter.

2 Connect the rays with a series of curved lines, reminiscent of a spider web.

3 Color the pattern with greens, red, and orange.

4 Outline the letter in orange.

fig. A

breathe in, breathe out

This piece is a reminder to breathe, take your time, and that everything will be okay. I began by drawing the words "breathe in breathe out" in pencil, and then traced over them with a black pen. I colored in the words, and then drew an outline in blue around them. I filled in the outline with yellow, green, and orange markers, and then I drew another blue outline around the first one. I filled in that space with small blue lines. Lastly, I drew a bunch of lines out toward the edges with different colored markers and added the dots at the ends.

EXPLORING SIMPLICITY

The colorful style of my work is something that I've seen shining through since the time I was a small kid. I am definitely a maximalist in terms of style. Steve Jobs once said, "Simplicity is the ultimate sophistication." I really like that. And it makes me wonder whether trying out a more minimalist approach might be nice and refreshing. We'll see.

Now that I've completed this piece, I'm very intrigued by what our favorite words might say about us as people. I noticed that many of mine are places I want to travel to, and subjects/things I'm interested in. The words are also ones that have sounds that I love. It makes me wonder if my interest in the subject or place makes me love the sound of the word or vice versa. I started with the word "Morroco" at the top of the page, and then filled in the page randomly with my favorite words. The last word I drew was "Beirut" at the bottom of the page. I added the little star-like shapes in circles at the end.

Pam Garrison

www.pamgarrison.typepad.com

I remember receiving a calligraphy starter set as a child for Christmas. I was over the moon! Because I loved it so much, I was somewhat hesitant to use it. But use it I did, and I have been drawn to calligraphy tools and practice pads ever since.

FAVORITE LETTER

I prefer numbers to letters, but if I had to pick one letter, I would choose "A," then "O," then "S." These letters are pretty and lend themselves easily to different lettering styles.

FAVORITE WRITING INSTRUMENTS

When I want to do my prettiest script writing, I turn to my dip pens. I love using my dip pen nibs with an oblique holder and calligraphy ink. I love the feel of the pen and the sound of the scratch it makes on the paper. For everyday writing, I like the extra-fine Pilot Precise Grip pen, which is inexpensive and available at most office supply stores. It has a good consistent ink flow and dries quickly, allowing me to easily color in my lettering and doodling work.

Flower Power

A pretty little flower placed at the centers of the letters is what makes this alphabet so charming. And with the help of an eraser, you can place the flower exactly where you please.

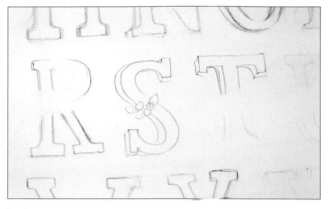

fig. A

fig. B

fig. C

WHAT YOU'LL NEED

* Pencil
* Hot-press paper
* Eraser
* Black fine-point monoline marker
* Colored markers

TECHNIQUE

1 Sketch Roman-style block letters with a pencil. Sketch additional lines on the left and lower portion of each letter to create dimension.

2 Decide where you want to place the flowers, and erase those spots on the letters. Sketch a small flower on the erased spots on each letter (**fig. A**).

3 Trace the letters and the flowers with a fine-point black marker (**fig. B**).

4 Erase the pencil marks.

5 Color the letters and flowers with colored markers (**fig. C**).

Outside-In Lettering

Lettering is a big part of the many art journals that I love to keep. This method of creating a colorful background, and then making "outside-in" lettering on top of the background, is something I do frequently in my art journals. It takes patience and time, but the results are wonderful.

fig. A

fig. B

fig. C

WHAT YOU'LL NEED

* Black fine-point monoline marker
* Watercolor paper
* Colored markers
* Watercolors
* Gray, pink, red, and black acrylic paints
* Paintbrush

TECHNIQUE

1 Doodle flowers and shapes onto watercolor paper with a fine-point black marker.

2 Fill in the doodles with colored markers. Fill in the rest of the page with watercolor paints and markers so that the entire page is filled with lots of shapes and colors. Note: Most of the doodles will be covered up with the lettering, so don't worry if they don't look perfect. The most important thing is to fill the page with many different shapes and colors (fig. A).

3 Visualize the words that you want to add. Paint the shape of the block letters for the first word with gray acrylic paint and a paintbrush. Do not outline or sketch the letters beforehand. Just visualize and paint, so that the letters can look playfully imperfect. Paint around the outside space of the letters to form a painted shape, perhaps a wonky oval or a rectangle.

4 Repeat step 3 to paint the rest of the words for the page. Let dry.

5 Paint over the gray word shapes with pink paint, allowing a slight portion of the gray paint at the edge of the letters to peek through. Let dry (fig. B).

6 Paint over the pink paint with red paint, allowing a slight portion of the gray and pink paint at the edge of the letters to peek through. Let dry.

7 Add small accents to the word shapes with black and gray paints (fig. C).

pam garrison 33

To keep track of some of my favorite hand-drawn letters, I created this book by tearing, folding, and stitching together four layers of watercolor paper. Each spread allows room for me to sketch in and color some of my favorite letters. It's a book that is fun to keep adding to, and one that I open up when I am in need of ideas for a project.

PLAY, PRACTICE, EXPERIMENT

For me, the blank white page opens up opportunities and possibilities. It's like a fresh start, a blank slate. I approach the page as play, which allows me not to worry about perfection or finishing an idea. It's all about active and creative discovery. Even when I am doing lettering projects for hire, like designing someone's logo, I permit myself important playtime to practice and experiment. I sketch out letters so that I can see what might eventually result from the experimenting.

This alphabet utilizes a concept similar to Flower Power (page 30). However, rather than starting with Roman-style block letters with serifs, I began by making simple sans serif ribbon-like letters. Then I erased parts of the letters and added doodled flowers and leaves. Some leaves and flowers could just be added at end points without having to erase.

François Bégnez

www.francoisbegnez.com

I was born with a pen in my hand! I drew comic strips when I was younger and often had to start with the title, so I loved drawing letters from the beginning. As a kid, I had no idea how my art would evolve. By the time I was 17 years old, when I started art school, I made a decision to experience new techniques while at the same time try hard to differentiate myself from these techniques and to develop my own style. This decision came to me one night when I realized that in order to be great, you have to become more independent and therefore unique.

FAVORITE WRITING INSTRUMENTS

I typically do not use pencils or ballpoint pens. I prefer using felt-tip pens. My favorite ones are the Mitsubishi Sign Pen and the Pilot Hi-Tecpoint V7 Grip. They're sweet.

FAVORITE LETTER

My favorite letter is "A," because it needs to go up, down, and horizontally. It contains all the moves! I also love the "W" and the "&" because they allow me to add curves and waves.

Le Vif Zephyr

For this composition, I created what I call multiple entrances: assorted clusters of words and letters made in varying sizes and styles. These multiple entrances allow me to more easily use improvisation to fill the rest of the space on the page. To me, works like these are never really finished.

fig. A

fig. B

fig. C

fig. D

fig. E

TECHNIQUE

1 Create one entrance by making sans serif letters and filling in the enclosed section of the letter "e." Create a second entrance by creating the word "over" with ornate serif letters (**fig. A**).

2 Add a third entrance with line letters that are more contemporary in style (**fig. B**).

3 Use different pens to create many other entrances with letters, numbers, symbols, and doodles (**fig. C**).

4 Go back to the entrances and use improvisation to react to what you see on the page. Fill in and decorate what has been created and gradually fill the entire page (**fig. D**).

5 If there are parts that you don't like, "erase" that portion by covering it up completely with a black marker (**fig. E**).

HESITATION, FEAR, STRESS

I've never been gripped with fear of the blank page. However, I do think a degree of hesitation is part of the creative process. It's that point right before you start creating and you don't know what will happen. Though I've not been known to feel fear, I frequently feel stress due to deadlines. Sometimes, the stress of deadlines can block me.

françois bégnez   39

la liste de courses

These words were created by using blue and orange markers. It is a pretty simple process that can generate many interesting types of letters.

1 For the word "sucre," I created block letters and used orange (for the most part) on the left part of the letters and blue on the right part of the letters.

2 For the first word in "Electric Guitar," I used the orange marker for the vertical strokes and the blue marker for the horizontal strokes. Then I did exactly the opposite for the second word.

3 For the word "Cruiser," I used the orange marker for the top portion of the letters and the blue marker for the lower portion of the letters.

4 Lastly, I created other words using the two markers. The key to success is to experiment and try out different ideas.

SCHOOLED AND EXPERIMENTAL

Everybody needs to be convinced that they are doing the right thing, and school sometimes helps with this. But I strongly believe that experimenting—a process where you're not sure whether you're doing the right thing—is important. Ultimately, getting schooled with the traditional methods and personal experimentation go hand-in-hand. They are complementary.

THIS WEEK → SUCRE
LAIT COMPLET
jus de fruits
ROUG
œufs œUFS viande
LESSIVE CONFITUR
CRUISER SKATEBO
ARD
ELECTRIC
GUITAR fleuris 3D

I used a Pentel black sign pen to create this alphabet. I didn't have to use a pencil before using the pen because I have been practicing similar letters for a while in my sketchbooks. The number "3" is—I don't know—not what I should have drawn but I think in the end, it goes with the rest, so I'm okay with it.

Here are some random pages from my assorted sketchbooks. These pages are where I experiment with letters and shapes and doodles. The less fancy the sketchbook, the more freedom there is to be experimental and get all ideas onto paper. Any sort of pen will do. One mark usually leads to another and before you know it, a new lettering style can emerge. Keep in mind that the only way you'll fill a sketchbook with ideas is to have it, along with a pen, close by you at all times.

jeffrey g. show

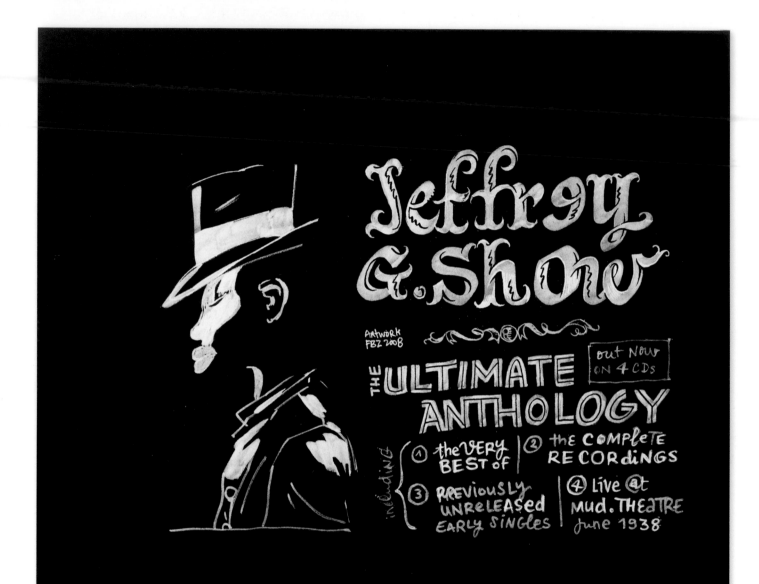

For this piece, I used white paint markers in different sizes and a CD marker on black paper. Some of the white lines were a bit transparent, so I had to go over them a second time. This created some volume on the letters. On some letters, I came back with a strong black pencil to add interesting details and to remove uninteresting white parts. I hope there will be a Blues artist who will see this work and immediately want me to design his next album cover.

This piece is a tribute to a Jimi Hendrix song, "The Wind Cries Mary." I like to draw the words of what I'm listening to or thinking of. I started this piece by making medium lines, then added bolder lines, and then finished with fine pencil work for the details.

Karyn Denten

www.den10studio.com

I studied graphic design in college. Back then, for our assignments, we had to hand letter everything. We enlarged letters from typography books on copy machines and literally cut and pasted letters together to form words. Looking back, this is probably where I learned to embrace the shapes of individual letters. Though the field of graphic design has evolved over time with the advances of technology, I've come to view the process of drawing the actual letters as a form of meditation.

FAVORITE WRITING INSTRUMENT

When I was in college studying graphic design, I used a technical pencil, but now a No. 2 Ticonderoga will do! A fine-point monoline marker by Pigma Micron is my favorite ink pen to use, especially the sizes .05 and .03. Those particular weights create perfect thin lines that are indicative of my style of "open face serif."

FAVORITE LETTER

My favorite letter is "E," uppercase or lowercase. I love the round side of the lowercase "e" and the straight line that forms the rest. Also, an uppercase "E" can be round or straight and either way can look elegant or strong, with great personality.

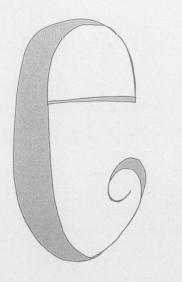

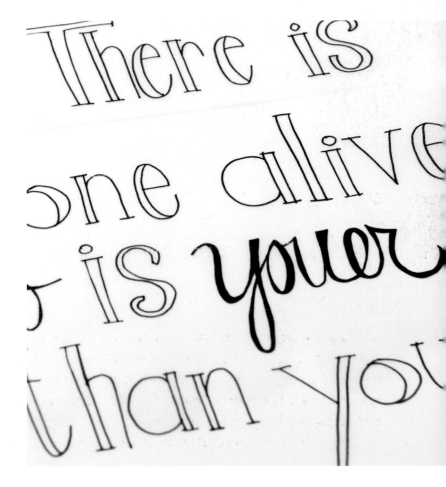

Sketch. Trace. Scan. Color. (Repeat as Needed)

I love the organic, irregular lines of my lettering and I don't want the computer to ever take that away, but I do use the computer to add color to my finished art pieces. I don't retrace anything digitally so I can maintain the hand-drawn look and style. To achieve letters in my style, which I describe as "open face serif" (see Serif and Sans Serif Defined on the next page), all you really need is a black monoline marker, either in size .05 or .03. You can leave the letters as is, or choose your favorite method to add color to the piece. Using Photoshop to add color is another option, which is what I like to use for my lettered pieces.

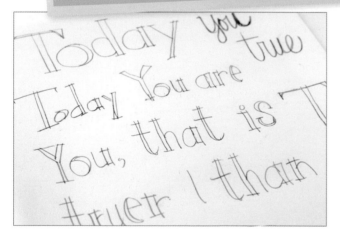

Today *you* are you, that is truer than true. There is no one alive who is *your* than you.

— *Dr. Seuss*

fig. A

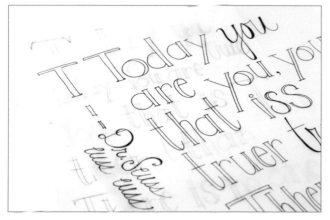

fig. B

WHAT YOU'LL NEED

* Pencil
* Scratch paper
* Black fine-point monoline marker
* Vellum
* Scanner
* Computer with Photoshop software
* Printer

TECHNIQUE

1 Lightly sketch letters onto a piece of scratch paper with a pencil. Start with the strokes to create the stems and then add the other lines to complete the letters **(fig. A)**.

2 Place a piece of vellum onto the scratch paper and trace the letters with a fine-point monoline marker **(fig. B)**.

3 Scan the traced vellum and then open up the scan on your computer, using Photoshop.

4 Use Photoshop to add color either in the letters' stems, or the background, or any other flourishes that you have sketched.

5 Size and print.

SERIF AND SANS SERIF DEFINED

Serif is a small line, curve, flourish, or detail projecting from the main part of a letter. Times New Roman is an example of a serif typeface.

Times New Roman

Sans Serif refers to letters that do not contain any details projecting from the main part of the letter. Helvetica is an example of a sans serif typeface.

Helvetica

I wrote "smile" in a lot of different styles. I didn't expect it to become a collection but it turned out as a nice study. I love variations of the same thing. The yellow, gray, and white form a simple yet eye-catching palette.

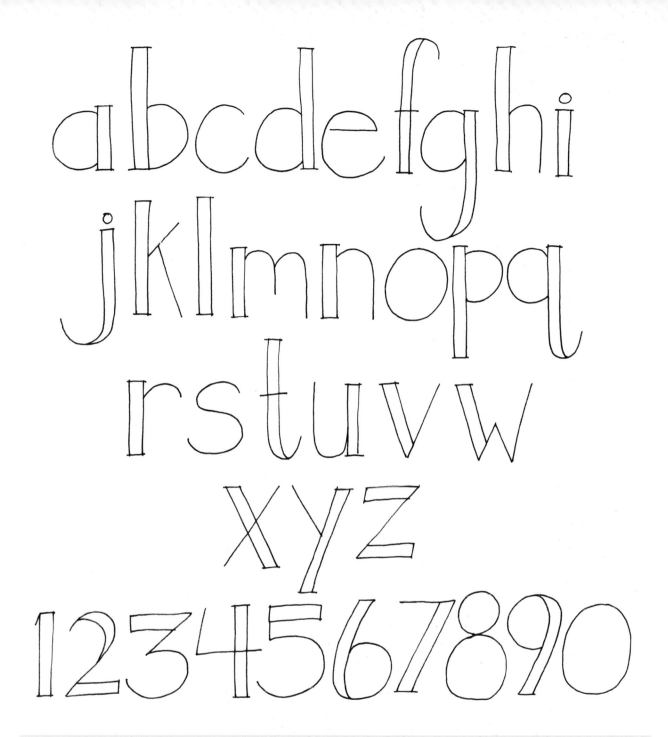

This lowercase alphabet is a simple one made with a fine-point black marker using thin, even strokes. Most of the letters have added lines to create chunky stems, which are great places to add color. There is a handful of letters that do not have the extra lines for chunky stems, just to keep things a little different and interesting.

Aimee Dolich

www.artsyville.blogspot.com

I'm big on combining methods, but not in a complicated way. I do some black-and-white lettering, but most of it is enhanced by color in some way, usually with an inked or watercolor background. The reason I combine coloring with my lettering is because the blank white paper unsettles me. It's like a blank canvas and seems to expect a lot of me, and I get worked up over the possibility of not being able to deliver. So I get over this by adding color—either inks or watercolors—to my page. Since something is already there, I don't feel like I'm having to create from scratch. The patterns and textures in the color give me a place to start.

FAVORITE LETTER

Oh, I love all letters! If hard-pressed to say, I guess it would have to be the letter "A," since that's the first letter of my first name and the first letter of my business: Artsyville.

FAVORITE WRITING INSTRUMENT

Permanent black markers by Staedtler, Copic, and Micron are my mainstays. I've experimented with every marker I can find, and these are the ones that give me the most control over my lines. They dry quickly, which is important; I am impatient and I don't like to wait for ink to dry. The ink from these markers tend to "sit" on the paper rather than bleed into them.

aimee dolich   53

A Human Was Here

My signature lettering method is pretty simple. I start by adding a wash of color, sketch letters on top of the color, and then plump the letters up. Through this simple process, there is always a playful, cheerful mood that gets cast, where the joy of the handwritten letter takes center stage. I have a strong passion for the individuality that is expressed in any kind of handwriting. Whether it is intended to be artful or not, it is all artful to me because it reveals (or invites questions) about the person who put the marks on the paper.

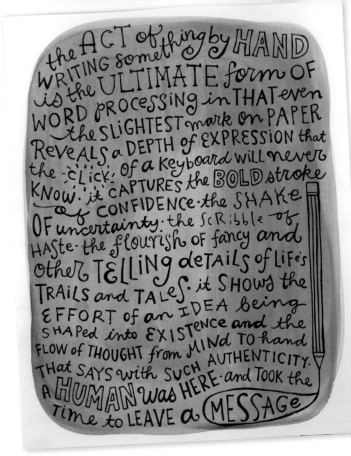

WHAT YOU'LL NEED

* Watercolors
* Hot-pressed 140 lb watercolor paper
* Mechanical pencil, .07mm
* Black permanent markers and ink pens, both fine and medium points
* Eraser

TECHNIQUE

1 Apply a wash of watercolor onto the watercolor paper and let it dry.

2 Lightly letter the words using a mechanical pencil. Create some with chunky stems, others with no stems, and others with playful swirls.

3 Trace the penciled letters with a black marker.

4 Trace over the letters again, in detail, "plumping up" some areas to give the letter more depth, and leaving other parts narrow. Use a combination of markers, types, and widths.

5 Erase any visible pencil marks.

6 When working on a larger piece, create letters in many different styles, including words in all uppercase, words in all lowercase, blocked letters, cursive letters, shaky letters, and at times, even a doodled pencil.

MIX AND COMBINE

Unless you wish to perfect a particular lettering technique, don't feel obligated to follow a font, style, or letterform line-for-line. I mix uppercase and lowercase freely, mix serifs and sans serifs freely, combine cursive and script with block letters, and rarely form two letters exactly the same way.

places TO find INSPIRATION for LETTERING YOUR WORDS by hAND

in SHAPES
TRees. clouds.
FLOWERS. PATTERNS
food. CARS.
shadows. MS
DREAMS

On the STREET
Billboards.
MOM & POP shop
SIGNS. graffiti.
POSTERS. Daily
SPECIAL menus

FROM the PAST
Album COVERS.
Vintage MAGAZINES
gift WRAP
CHAPBOOKS.
manuscripts

FROM the HEART
Handwritten
LETTERS
& CHILDREN's
ARt

I adapted this work from a handwritten brochure I designed for a guest lecture in typography at the University of Kansas. The students were working on a special segment of hand typography, and I set them loose on multiple lettering exercises, encouraging them to look beyond traditional stock fonts for their inspiration.

This "plumped up" alphabet has lots of swirls. The spirit of this alphabet is one that invites you to customize the size and relationship with the other letters, depending on the project that you are working on. I consider the alphabet one of my favorite art tools!

Andy Ainger

www.andyainger.com

According to my parents, I was happy as a child to sit for hours, drawing the world around me. I'm sure that soon after learning to speak and spell, typography started making appearances in my drawings. I can remember my dad creating signs for his workplace, using thick marker pens. I was always amazed by how clean and consistent he could make the letters. This has inspired me tremendously, from an early age, to create hand-drawn typography.

FAVORITE WRITING INSTRUMENTS

I primarily use a pencil to draft out my ideas onto paper. After I have decided on my idea, I normally draw with a fine-line ink pen (something between 0.3 to 0.7 nib size) or a brush, depending on the effect I want to achieve or surface I'm working on. Sometimes I'll re-draw the same design over and over again using layout paper or tracing paper until I'm totally happy with the forms and letters.

FAVORITE LETTER

"A" is my favorite letter, because it makes both my initials.

Highlighted and Doodled

This is a fun method that allows you to make some very cool letters with just a plain old highlighter and a black fine-point marker.

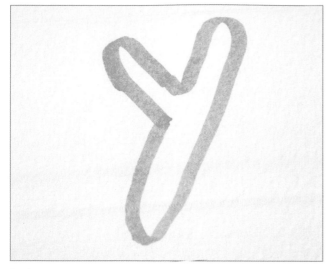

fig. A

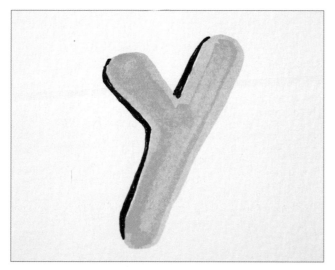

fig. B

fig. C

TECHNIQUE

1 Lightly sketch the outline of a letter with a pencil. Trace over the outline with a highlighter pen and let dry. Erase the pencil marks with an eraser (**fig. A**).

2 Color in the outline with the highlighter. Create a shadow by creating thin lines on the left and lower sides of the letter with a black fine-point marker. Color in this space with the marker (**fig. B**).

3 Use the marker to doodle small lines and curves in the body of the highlighted letter (**fig. C**).

OLD AND THE NEW

I am constantly trying new mediums and methods, often combining them with older, more favorite techniques and tools. I will often use traditional methods in conjunction with computer software. For me, it's important to have fun with the work. This juxtaposition allows the work to become something more unique and different.

Andy's Bug Alphabet

Once you get the hang of creating little chunky bugs, it's all about arranging them with other small doodles to compose the letters.

fig. A   fig. B

fig. C   fig. D

WHAT YOU'LL NEED

* Pencil
* Sketchbook
* Black fineliner pen
* Scanner
* Computer with Photoshop software
* Printer

TECHNIQUE

1 Doodle a puffy little bug (**fig. A**).

2 Give the bug some food by doodling some tiny flowers and leaves (**fig. B**).

3 Invite more bugs to join the fun by doodling additional bugs to further shape the letter (**fig. C**).

4 Add more food for the friends by doodling more flowers and leaves (**fig. D**).

5 Create the rest of the alphabet by doodling bugs and bug food.

6 Scan the alphabet, digitally color the letters in Photoshop, and print.

ENCOURAGING MISTAKES

Doodling in sketchbooks is a great way of discovering techniques and creating ideas. It's part of the process I've always used. I like to encourage mistakes, and I love the sudden rush of creative adrenaline when new techniques start coming together on a page. I find working in this way often results in more expressive and interesting works being created.

all about "a"

I found this wooden "A" shape in a local charity shop and decided to give it a facelift. After removing the old paint with sandpaper, I applied several undercoats of a white matte spray paint. Once the coats were dry, I started to carefully paint patterns on each side, using acrylic paint and small paintbrushes.

This doodled "A" is one I made in my sketchbook. I first outlined the letter shape in pencil, then used a black fine-point marker to doodle faces, shapes, and lines into the letter's space. Once the doodling was done, I traced the outline of the letter, mindful of capturing the spirit of some of the doodles in the outline—such as having a wisp of hair on the left side swoosh out from the outline, and allowing the cat's paws to protrude from the lower left part of the letter shape.

Here is a page filled with all sorts of As: uppercase, lowercase, serif, sans serif, block lines, fat, thin, tall, short, and more.

This piece uses the Futura typeface as the basis for each letter shape. Once I sketched the letters with pencil, I doodled in the letters' space with a black fine-point marker. Washes of watercolor were added to the letters and to the background.

mean to go on

After I drew the letter shapes with a black marker, I added shadows, lines within the letters, and then the lines and doodles beyond the letters to connect them all together.

Once I decided on the phrase "hold me tight," it was great fun adding the hands to the lower part of the "H" and the upper part of the "T," to have the letters help capture the spirit of the words.

andy ainger 67

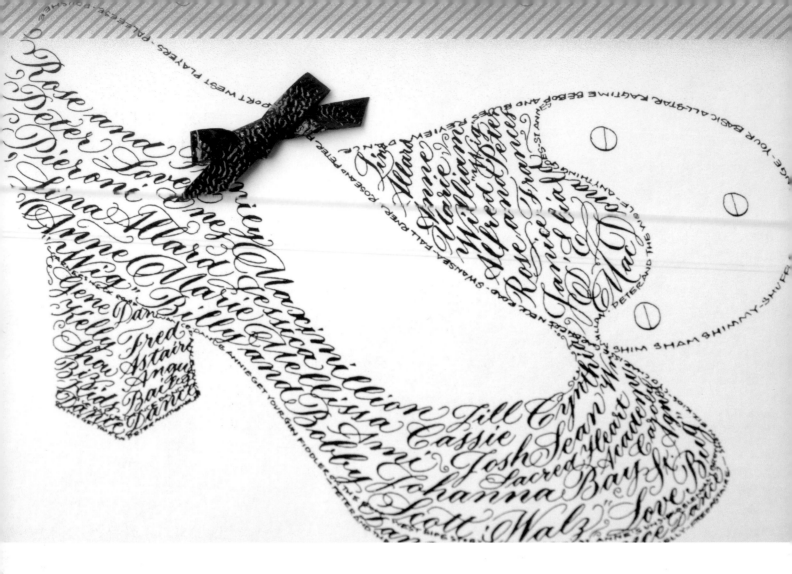

Linda Schneider

www.lindaschneiderart.com

Even when I was a young child, my hands could never stay still. I drew on walls, furniture, anywhere I could make a mark. I remember being in trouble in kindergarten when I would draw outside the lines; so I began my creativity at a young age and missed numerous recesses because of that. It has paid off now, as it is the air under my wings that makes me soar to new levels, and I love it. I knew I was hooked on the art of lettering when I realized that I was noticing the letter formations first, along with the positive and negative spaces that letters create, before reading the meaning of the words.

FAVORITE WRITING INSTRUMENTS

My favorite calligraphic tool is a pointed pen, consisting of a pen holder, either straight or oblique, and nib. Speedball has inexpensive black pen holders that are good to start with, and I recommend the Hunt 56 nib to use with the holder. I also really like the Pentel brush-tip sign pen. It is a marker-style pen with a brush on the end, which allows you to make thick or thin lines depending on your pressure and release.

FAVORITE LETTER

My favorite letter is "L," because I have practiced it the most. My maiden name was Linda Lee Leeming.

Pictorial Calligraphy

The pressure and release methods used to create letters can also be applied to make what I call "pictorial calligraphy"—doodles that complement pointed pen work. The doodles can be small flowers, leaves, or simple patterns. They can even be shoes!

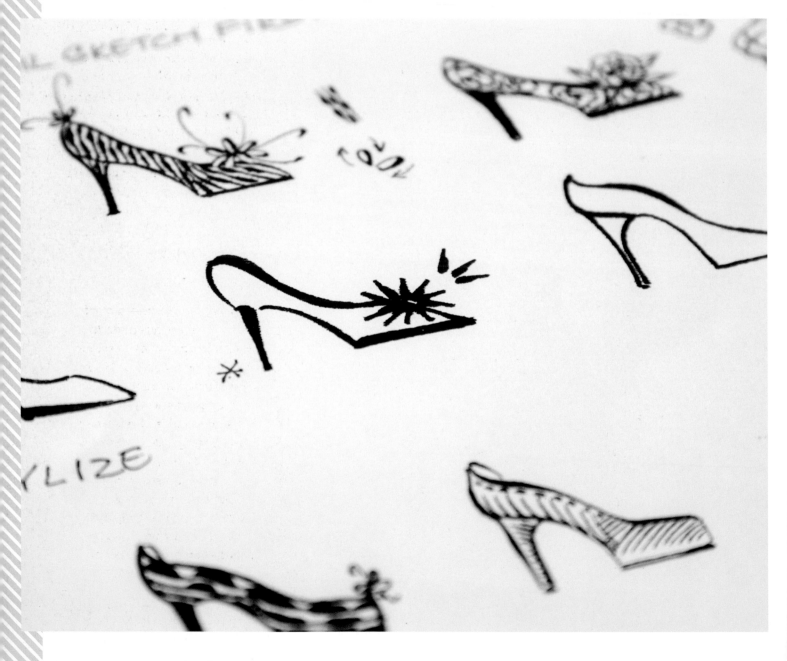

fig. A

fig. B

fig. C

WHAT YOU'LL NEED

* Pencil
* Paper
* Pointed or brush-tip pen
* Eraser
* Black ink
* Watercolors or colored markers

TECHNIQUE

1 Draw a simple shoe shape with a pencil **(fig. A)**.

2 Trace over the drawing with a pointed pen with pressured downstrokes to create thicks and released upstrokes to create thins **(fig. B)**.

3 Fill in the shape, using the same pressure and release methods to create assorted doodles and designs **(fig. C)**.

4 Erase wayward pencil marks.

5 Add color with watercolors or colored markers.

MY STYLE

Not a day goes by that I am not drawn to my calligraphy desk, where I find pleasure and escape. Once my pen is dipped into the ink and glides across the paper, I've found that sweet place in life. I've tripped and fallen a few times in learning my calligraphic steps, but I found pleasure in practicing, and that was the secret to success. Often my process involves making my calligraphic strokes while accompanied by classical music, with a piece of dark chocolate by my side.

linda schneider   71

Lines using pressure ↘ release ↗

Brush Spencerian

A B C D
E F G H I
J K L M
N O P Q
R S T U V
W X Y Z

a b c d e f g h i

j k l m n o p q r

s t u v x y z

Pressure and release are the fundamental components in making thin and thick strokes with a pointed pen. Generally, when the pen is on an upstroke, you release the pressure of the pen to create a thin line. When the pen is on a downstroke, you add pressure to the pen to create a thick line. These are the principles I have used to develop the uppercase and lowercase Spencerian script alphabets shown here.

The same pressure and release methods were used to create this goddess figure, juxtaposed with a hand-lettered word.

TAPED TOOTHPICKS

The most unusual lettering tool I've used is the toothpick. Actually, I taped five toothpicks together so that I could use them to make a musical clef. Once the clef was made, I created notes on the clef. This was actually for a card project I did for Papyrus stationery stores.

Lori Vliegen

www.elviestudio.blogspot.com

When I was a little girl, my mom and I used to color at night before I went to bed. One night she taught me how to write my name using one of my crayons. I went to bed dreaming of how fun that was, to be able to draw those letters. Come to think of it, I still go to bed dreaming of drawing fun letters! I am attracted to lettering not just because the forms are fun to make, but also because the process can be quite therapeutic.

FAVORITE WRITING INSTRUMENTS

I have a collection of Micron and Pitt pens that are starting to take over my studio! They come in a variety of nib sizes, and the ink is archival and highly pigmented, making them really easy to use for lettering and experimenting. What I like best is that they are easy to find at my local craft store. When I'm not relying on my pens, I love to use a perfectly mixed deep black gouache, or a diluted thimble-full of Dr. Ph. Martin's Bleed Proof White, which looks beautiful on a piece of black paper.

FAVORITE LETTER

I love writing a cursive capital "L." Those loop-de-loops are SO much fun to play with.

Color Your World

In many of my lettered works, you can find the hand that I've developed over the years, something I call "Elvie Cursive." It's great on its own, and also when combined with other types of lettering and doodles. In this piece, I incorporated this lettering method with colorful thumbprints. The idea was inspired by a class I took with Alisa Burke, who encouraged us to create a color wheel.

fig. A

fig. B

WHAT YOU'LL NEED

* Pencil
* Paper
* Black fine-point monoline marker
* Eraser
* Paper stump (see page 80)
* Round lid or template
* Pigment inkpads, assorted colors
* Watercolors

TECHNIQUE

1 Write the central words in cursive on a piece of paper, using a pencil.

2 Draw parallel strokes on the parts of the letter that feel naturally to be downstrokes, to build them up. Do not add strokes to parts of the letter that feel like upstrokes (**fig. A**).

3 Trace over the pencil lines with a fine-point monoline marker. Erase any remaining pencil lines, and color in the built-up areas with the marker (**fig. B**).

4 Add soft shading around each letter using a pencil and paper stump (see How to Use a Paper Stump on page 80).

5 Using a pencil, trace around a plate, lid, or a circle template to sketch a large circle beyond the lettered area.

6 Sketch scallops around the circle with a pencil. Add strokes to parts of the scallop to build it up. Trace over the pencil lines with a fine-point monoline marker and erase any remaining pencil lines.

7 Stamp your thumbprint onto the paper with a pigment inkpad. Repeat with different inkpad colors, making sure to clean your thumb in between colors.

8 Add facial features, arms, and legs to the thumbprints, as well as simple lettering and flourishes around the scallops, using a fine-point monoline marker.

9 Add color to the scallops and small color-sample dots using watercolors.

The word "sunlight" was created using my signature lettering technique, and a pencil and paper stump for the shading. The other words were made with simple, non-ornamental lines, so that the piece would feel light and fun. My original sketch included a scallop border around the outside edge. Once I saw everything in color, I decided to stick with the blue and yellow checkerboard design to keep it simple.

SILENCING THE INNER CRITIC

Many people, especially when just starting out, become overly self-critical of their work. I think that lettering is no different than painting, sewing, photography, or any other artform. It takes time and practice to develop your own style, and the courage to do so, even in the presence of the pesky inner critic.

Aa Bb Cc Dd
Ee Ff Gg Hh
Ii Jj Kk Ll
Mm Nn Oo Pp
Qq Rr Ss Tt
Uu Vv Ww Xx
Yy Zz
0 1 2 3 4 5 6 7 8 9

I would describe the style of my alphabet as a chunky cursive. As long as you know how to write words in cursive, you can create this hand. After you have written a letter, you'll want to go back in and add strokes to create and fill the thicker portions of the letters. Once you get the hang of it, you'll see how fun and easy it is.

HOW TO USE A PAPER STUMP

A paper stump looks like a pencil, but is made of tightly rolled-up gray paper felt that has been sharpened on the end (sometimes both ends) to resemble pencil points. A paper tortillion is the same as a paper stump, except it is slightly shorter and thinner for detailed work. Use the points to blend and smudge marks made with pencils, pastels, and charcoals. To keep the ends pointy, the paper stump can be sharpened on a sanding block.

This artwork was inspired by my friend Rynda, who loves artichokes. I think it would look nice framed and hanging in a kitchen. The letters were made using my signature Elvie Cursive method. The artichoke was painted using watercolor pencils. The border and other tiny details and accents were made with a fine-point monoline marker.

LEARNING THE RULES FIRST

Experimental lettering is great fun and the results can be fantastic. However, I think there's a lot to be said for learning the rules first, and then you'll know how to break the rules properly. I'm a huge fan of seeking the best instruction possible by reading books, attending classes, and viewing the works of skilled lettering artists, so I can build a strong lettering foundation.

Madeline Tompkins
(with Diane Tompkins)

www.tagteamtompkins.etsy.com

I remember a 7th grade math class being so uninteresting that I spent every second the teacher wasn't peering over my shoulder working on a new handwriting style. I was shocked when I got a test back and she had given me a bad grade because she couldn't read my "new" handwriting. So I went back and refined it enough to make us both happy. Muscle memory is so important for hand lettering. But that doesn't mean that everything that comes out of a beginner is unsatisfactory. I love seeing what newbies do. When someone doesn't know "the rules" of lettering, sometimes the results can be pleasantly raw and unexpected.

FAVORITE LETTER

I really do enjoy the letter "G," uppercase and lowercase. I have a few favorite ways of lettering the uppercase "G" and it's sometimes hard to decide which style I like best for the piece I'm working on. And then there's the lowercase "g" … which begs the question: Who doesn't love a good descender?!

FAVORITE WRITING INSTRUMENT

After playing around with dozens of different flexible nibs for my dip pens, I fell upon a Japanese nib (Deleter Comic Pen: G-Pen 240) that is strong enough to hold up to my strong touch and yet flexible enough to get all the thicks and thins I desire in my work. It's so strong that I've been working with the same one for months without having to switch it out.

Nevermore

My signature lettering is frequently paired with my mom's (Diane Tompkins) fabulous silhouette paper-cutting methods. The parts that each of us create are different, and we definitely have to have good communication early on, for the piece to turn out smoothly. This piece illustrates how we combine our processes.

* Pencil
* Scratch paper
* Black printmaking paper (for silhouette)
* Masking tape
* Self-healing cutting mat
* Sharp craft knife
* 100 percent pure rough rag marker paper (for rough lettering sketch)
* Dip pen holder and nib
* Black waterproof ink
* Hot-press watercolor paper
* Light box
* Xyron machine with permanent film adhesive

TECHNIQUE

1 Create a rough sketch of the intended silhouette and lettering.

2 Place the final sketch on top of the black paper and secure in place with masking tape at the top and bottom areas. Place these layers of paper on top of a self-healing cutting mat (**fig. A**).

3 Carefully and patiently cut the silhouette of the sketch through both layers of paper, using a sharp craft knife. Set aside (**fig. B**).

4 Practice the lettering on a piece of rough rag marker paper with a dip pen and black waterproof ink.

5 Select the best rough rag piece and place it on a light box. Place a piece of hot press watercolor paper on top of the rough rag and lightly pencil in the lettering.

6 Letter over the pencil marks with a dip pen and black waterproof ink. Let dry.

7 Erase pencil marks. Apply film adhesive to the backside of the silhouette and affix in place. Splatter ink on top by flicking a nib loaded with ink with your fingernails.

fig. A

fig. B

madeline tompkins 85

From ghoulies and ghosties, And long-leggedy beasties, And things that go bump in the night, Good Lord, deliver us.

SCOTTISH PROVERB

This was a tricky quote to finish because of its length, and because of the many ascenders and descenders involved. I had to sketch this one out many times to get the flow just right. I had fun pulling out some of the words and phrases to letter. It was much easier to letter the quote in parts and pieces instead of all at the same time. This enabled me to concentrate on the individual look of the words.

After lettering the quote, I lettered it a second time to use in our letterpress piece. I learned enough the first time so the second time wasn't as hard. I just needed to clean it up digitally and place it within the silhouette that my mom cut.

HOURS OPENING DRAWERS

Growing up with an artist mother, there was always plenty of art supplies around the house. And she was kind enough to share with a child who probably wasn't very kind to her expensive brushes. She had an old dentist's chest that she put most of her art supplies in and I would spend hours opening all the little drawers, pulling out pencils, pens, pastels, inks, and brushes to play with.

I'm going to go out on a limb and say that my signature lettering style, as reflected in this alphabet, can be classified as "Lighthearted Gothic." It is created with a dip pen and nib with general principles of lettering applying: where the hand is heavy on the downstrokes to create the thicks, and light on the upstrokes to create the thins. The Lighthearted Gothic comes into play with the smallest details, like the exaggerated swirls, the scribbly dots for the lowercase "I" and "J," and the pointy crescent-shapes found in other letters, such as the "G" and "Z."

dire Warning #51

"Beer and Whiskey, mighty risky."

m + d tompkins

My mom and I have done several of these "Dire Warnings" before, so we've established the overall look of the series. After lettering and adhering the silhouette came my favorite part: the splattering. If I splatter too much, I end up with a big ink drop in a bad spot, obscuring an important part of the piece. If I don't splatter enough, it doesn't have the impact that I am looking for.

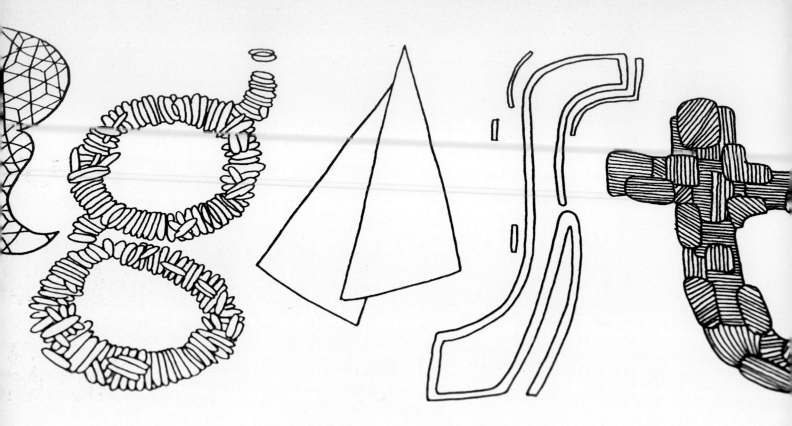

Stine Kaasa

www.stinekaasa.org

Sometimes it can be hard to get started. Working with letters, you are often looking for something to write, and not having anything in particular to say makes it hard to get started at all. I often start making random letters, trying to think of each letter as shapes put together, not worrying too much about making words or meaning. Trying different techniques, such as writing with the non-dominant hand or blindfolded, can also work well. Such exercises deplete your sense of control, which takes away some of the pressure of making something perfect. With the pressure off, good things frequently surface.

FAVORITE LETTER

My favorite letter is "A." I like how the letter looks and also how the letter has so many variations. The uppercase "A" can look very different from a lowercase one, and it can be drawn in many different ways, both with rounded and angled shapes.

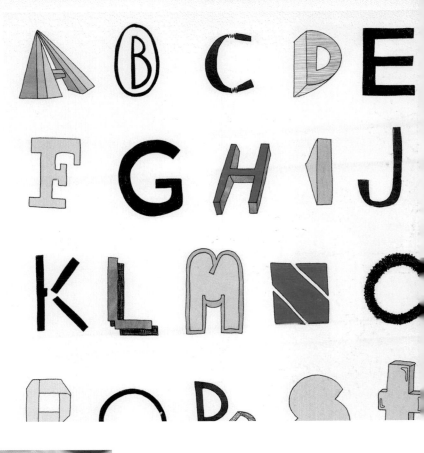

FAVORITE WRITING INSTRUMENTS

Although I do like to vary what sorts of tools I use, there are some that I always reach for. I often start out with pencils or fine liner pens. For color, I use Letraset ProMarkers, brush markers, Gelly Roll pens, or gouache paint. Fineliners are perfect for making details and patterns. I often sketch with a pencil, then use a light box, where I trace the lines afterward. Letraset ProMarkers give a nice, even color that you can increase by adding extra layers. It is perfect for making shades.

Make a Poster

This method explores the use of geometric shapes and the ways translucent papers can be cut and layered for different effects in color. There is no right or wrong when it comes to making these letters and there is plenty of room for experimentation.

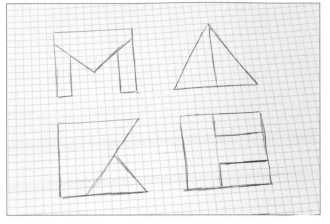

fig. A

fig. B

fig. C

WHAT YOU'LL NEED

* Graph paper
* Pencil
* Sharp craft knife
* Cutting mat
* Yellow and blue vellum
* White glue
* White paper

TECHNIQUE

1 Sketch letters onto graph paper with a pencil (**fig. A**).

2 Cut out the sketched letterforms with a sharp craft knife and cutting mat.

3 Use the cut graph paper as a starting point for developing simplified template shapes. Use these templates to cut out shapes from the yellow and blue translucent vellum papers.

4 Combine the cut shapes until you create a letter that you like (**fig. B**).

5 Use a bit of white glue to stick the pieces together and adhere them to a large piece of white paper. Be careful about the placement of the glue and try to apply it where there is a fold; otherwise, when the glue dries, it will show through the vellum (**fig. C**).

RECOGNIZING SELF

Even though my work has changed and developed over the years, I think my style does shine through—maybe not all the way back to my childhood, but at least throughout my adult years. I have found working methods that I am comfortable with. I like to develop and try new things, but often, if I try something that is too different from the way I normally work, I just feel like it does not look good, or I don't recognize myself in it.

Confetti Words

Patience is an important ingredient when creating letters using this method. It takes patience to punch holes of paper and to cut other small pieces of "confetti." Once the punched holes or other confetti shapes are made, it takes another dose of patience to adhere them carefully onto the paper.

fig. A

fig. B

WHAT YOU'LL NEED

* Pencil
* Heavyweight white paper
* Construction paper in assorted colors
* Paper hole punch
* Scissors
* Glue
* Eraser

TECHNIQUE

1 Sketch letters onto heavyweight paper with a pencil.

2 Create paper confetti with a hole punch, by punching out circles from construction paper. You can also use scissors to cut out wonky squares or triangles (**fig. A**).

3 Adhere punched confetti pieces to the inside of the sketched letters, or glue the pieces in the negative space of the sketched letters for a different effect. Let dry (**fig. B**).

4 Erase wayward pencil marks with an eraser.

MORE TO COME

During my education, I had access to letterpress printing and was encouraged to make my own letters using various materials. I also started looking at other designers who worked with handmade type, and found lots of inspiration. I feel there are still many things to discover about letters, and I have plenty of other methods I want to try out.

Here's a fun piece that combines three styles: one with tiny pink and fuchsia triangular shapes in the body of the letters, another with green and yellow blocks of color, and a third with very simple line drawings made with a purple marker.

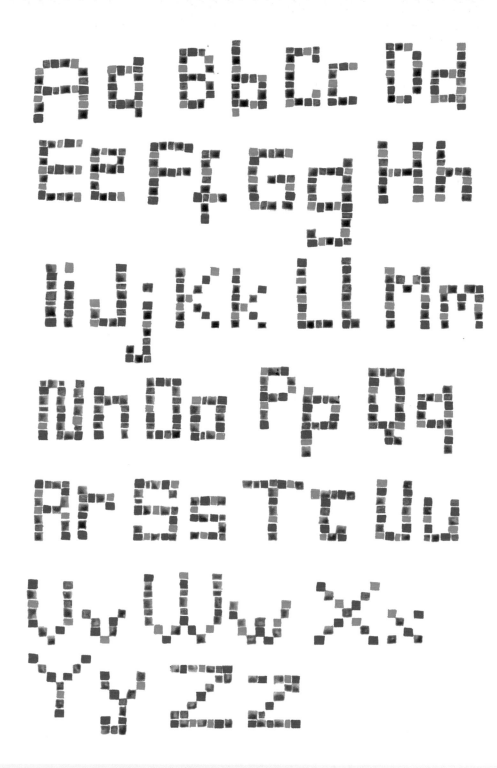

I started by sketching letters onto graph paper. Next, I redrew the final letter shapes onto a white sheet of paper, drawing all the squares separately. I then placed a new heavyweight piece of paper onto the sketched letters, put both layers onto a light box, and traced all the little squares. I used fine-point markers to color in each square.

These letters were made with just a plain black marker. It goes to show just how many different directions a single letter can go.

spend the day outside

For this piece, I started out by typing the text on the computer and printing it out. I traced the words onto a new sheet of paper, using a light box and a pencil. On the same sheet, I sketched out a few ideas for the background, to fill the negative space while leaving the letters blank, leaving the sketch on the light box, I started working on a new sheet of paper, adding sections of color to correspond with the background. I filled in one color at a time in all the places where I wanted that color to be.

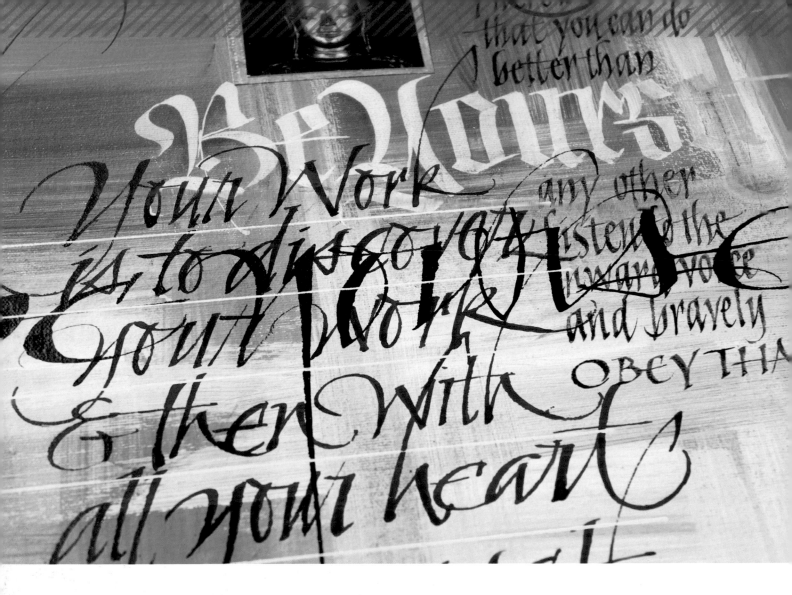

Lisa Engelbrecht

www.lisaengelbrecht.com

When I was about seven or eight, a neighbor friend showed me a piece of Eucalyptus bark on which she had written and doodled a flower. The writing was cute and curly and I decided that that's what I wanted to do. I started playing with my letters right then and there. I think lettering is at the heart of the soul and conveys emotion and character. Hand-lettered anything wins over type any day. Whose heart doesn't skip a beat when they see a handwritten letter or card from a loved one?

abcdefghijklm
nopqrstuvwxyz

abcdefghijklm
nopqrstuvwxyz

abcdefghijklm

FAVORITE WRITING INSTRUMENT

My favorite lettering tool of all time has to be the Parallel pen by Pilot. It is so versatile. It has a cartridge inside so I don't have to dip the nib into ink. But the cool thing is that I can also dip the nib into other inks and metallic powders to get interesting effects.

FAVORITE LETTER

The letter "L" is probably my favorite because I've dealt with it so many times with my name. It's simple and easy to add flourishes.

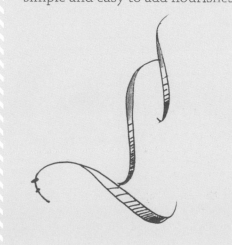

Letterista Script

Once you get the hang of this Letterista Script, which I designed, you'll see how fun it is to create words and add color to them. It's a pretty simple process. You just need a little practice.

fig. A

fig. B

fig. C

WHAT YOU'LL NEED

* Black fine-point marker
* Paper
* Sparkly gel pens

TECHNIQUE

1 Make clean simple strokes to create the base of the letter (**fig. A**).

2 Observe the letters and decide which parts are made with an upstroke and which parts are made with downstrokes. On the sections that are made with downstrokes, create a second parallel line to thicken the letter (**fig. B**).

3 In that thickened space, use the black marker to darken the lower part of the letter. Continue upward, making lines that are wider spaced toward the middle of the letter (**fig. C**).

4 Use steps 1–3 to letter a name or a quote.

5 Add color to the upper parts of the letters with an assortment of sparkly gel pens.

SWEET ON SUMI

Sumi ink is the best black ink for me. It has a luscious intensity and smooth flow. Some Sumi inks are scented with incense … oh, what fun to write with! I use Sumi ink for all my work for print. On fabric, I prefer using acrylic inks in great permanent colors that have lasting power on fabric.

Love Alphabet Blocks

These chunky canvas blocks pair well with the Kooky Alphabet (page 106) and are so fun to make! You could make one for each member of your family or make the entire alphabet to adorn a wall.

fig. A

fig. B

fig. C

WHAT YOU'LL NEED

* Canvas blocks
* White gesso
* Acrylic inks
* Paintbrushes
* Acrylic paints
* Soda can pen (see page 107)
* Old dictionary pages
* Matte medium

TECHNIQUE

1. Prime the canvas block by applying a coat of white gesso onto the surface. Let dry.

2. Select two or three colors of acrylic inks and apply them, one color at a time, to the primed canvas block. Let dry.

3. Paint a heart shape with a coordinating color of acrylic ink or acrylic paint. Let dry (**fig. A**).

4. With a soda can pen and acrylic ink, create a large letter that overlaps the heart. Add smaller words along the edges of the block (**fig. B**).

5. Cut out a word from an old dictionary page and adhere it to the block with matte medium (**fig. C**).

WEIRD TOOLS

I teach a class on weird tools. My students will often surprise me with something I would never have thought to use as a tool. Some examples include shims, a celery stalk, bamboo, Stim-U-Dent plaque remover sticks, sour cream containers, a cat whisker, road kill porcupine bristle brushes, straws, roofer's felt, carpenter's pencils, ruling pens, brushes made from whisk broom bristles, and branches … just to name a few!

ABC
DEFGH
IJKLMN
OPQR
STUV
WXYZ

These letters, which I call the Kooky Alphabet, were made with a homemade soda can pen. If you have a soda can, scissors, duct tape and a pencil, you can make a soda can pen and you can letter this alphabet (see the next page)!

HOW TO MAKE A SODA CAN PEN

The key to making a soda can pen is knowing that no two pens are exactly the same. Your nib will vary, depending on how subtle or severe you make the diagonal cut in step 3.

WHAT YOU'LL NEED

* Empty, clean soda can
* Scissors
* Pencil
* Duct tape (available in a range of decorative colors and patterns)
* Pipette or eyedropper

TECHNIQUE

1   Cut off the top and bottom from a soda can, then cut a line from top to bottom to open it up. Flatten out the metal and cut out a 2½-inch (6.4 cm) square **(fig. A)**.

2   Fold the square in half, and keep the folded edge on the right side. Cut out a small square from the lower left section of both layers. Each side of the small cutout square should be about ⅝ inch (1.6 cm). With the square cut out, you have now created the lower stem **(fig. B)**.

3   Cut from the lower left corner above the stem to the top right corner in a slightly curved diagonal. Cut both layers at the same time **(fig. B)**.

4   Place a sharpened pencil into the soda can nib and fasten the stem to the pencil with duct tape. Add another piece of duct tape to the lower middle section of the nib **(fig. C)**.

5   To use the soda can pen, load the nib with ink from the opening, using a pipette or eye dropper **(fig. D)**.

fig. A

fig. B

fig. C

fig. D

lisa engelbrecht   107

Philippe Debongnie

www.philippedebongnie.be

When I was 12 or 13, I drew a lot of logos. I think my love of lettering comes from this experience, of seeing nice brand logos and copying them. Prior to that, when I was eight or nine, I learned to draw in perspective—you know, with two or three points, the horizon line and all. I found it extremely interesting. Another time, I learned to draw geometric figures solely with a compass and a ruler. I spent hours drawing different shapes and coloring them out very precisely. I think all of these experiences fueled my fascination with letters. After all, letters are very definite structures and yet they have endless possibilities for variation. I could spend my whole life copying nice letters and exploring those in different ways.

FAVORITE WRITING INSTRUMENTS

The tools I use time and time again are watercolor, ballpoint pens, pencils, and Stabilo pens, in all sizes and colors. I also use scissors to cut out letters from old magazines, as well as other elements I can use with the letters for collage work.

FAVORITE LETTER

I don't have a favorite letter. I do like the "&" though. The French word for ampersand, which is "esperluette," is a poem in itself and really sings as a name.

Mapped Letters

This method is all about drawing letters inspired by favorite fonts, onto maps and then cutting out the letters. Once the letters are cut, they can be mounted onto paper, ready to be part of a larger composition with some drawing and collage. The thing to remember about this method is that you have to be ready to go along with any slip of the cutting knife. The letters are never going to be as nice or as straight as the original font that inspires the letters. But this imperfection is one of the reasons I like this technique.

fig. A

.fig. B

fig. C

WHAT YOU'LL NEED

* Map
* Pencil
* Sharp craft knife
* Cutting mat
* Glue stick
* Heavyweight paper
* Eraser

TECHNIQUE

1 Lightly sketch letters onto a map with a pencil.

2 Place the map onto a cutting mat and cut out the letters with a sharp craft knife **(fig. A)**.

3 Adhere the cut letters onto heavyweight paper and let dry **(fig. B)**.

4 Erase any wayward marks with an eraser.

5 If there are parts that you don't like, "erase" that portion by covering it up completely with a black marker **(fig. C)**.

Note: For the final work, I scanned the letters and combined them with my drawings and collage work digitally, in Photoshop.

Lego Letters

To make these letters, all you need is time to build the letters and a decent camera. I photographed mine against a white background with lots of light coming from the front. To create every letter and make them all different, I had to doodle some and figure out how many blocks high and how many blocks wide were needed.

fig. A

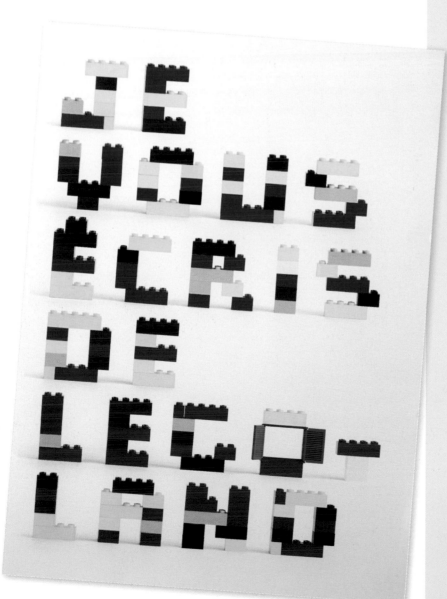

WHAT YOU'LL NEED

* Legos
* Camera
* White background with good lighting
* Computer with Photoshop software
* Printer

TECHNIQUE

1 Design and build letters using Legos **(fig. A)**.

2 Photograph each letter individually, against a white background.

3 Import the photos into Photoshop and compose the words.

4 Size and print.

EASY AND DIFFICULT

Lettering is simultaneously easy and difficult. It is easy because all you have to do is draw letters. We all know what letters look like, and they are not hard to draw or recognize. Then comes the hard part: How do you draw a good letter? How do you want that "a" to look? What do you want it to convey? Which font do you want to start with? Do you want it to have a fun side? Or do you want the letter to look really serious? What is the word? Is it legible the way you've drawn it? Are you sure? Letters are a finite number of figures with endless possibilities—so it's easy to draw them, but hard to feel like you did a good job. You always end up with more questions than when you started.

philippe debongnie 113

I have created several alphabets to share as follows:

* Chunky uppercase sans serif alphabet cut with scissors from old magazine pages and mounted onto paper.
* Simple sans serif lowercase alphabet made with tiny lines in graduated shades of colored markers.
* Simple sans serif lowercase alphabet made with watercolors and a small paintbrush.
* Uppercase serif alphabet drawn with a black fine-point marker and accented with horizontal lines made with a red marker.

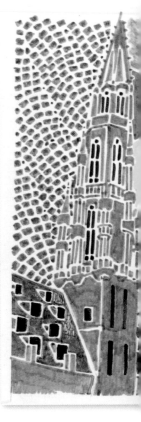

A simple sketch with a pencil is how I started this piece, creating basic shapes and composition. After that, I used a black fine-point marker to create many, many lines and curves that came out as I was working on it. The letters in the middle of the piece are made up of small lines. The letters toward the bottom of the piece are outlined and encased with small lines.

For this piece, I sketched the composition and the different elements with my pencils, and then I colored it with my markers. The many different styles of letters, as well as the many different buildings and colors, capture the essence of Brussels—a very chaotic city and a fun locale full of history and nice little places.

TOTALLY WORN OUT
AND LOUDLY
PROCLAIMING
WOW
what a ride

Barbara Close

www.bcdezigns.com

I was five years old when I got a Parker pen for my birthday. I loved it. I was so excited. Certainly from that point on, and perhaps before then, I have always loved letters and drawing. During high school, when my talent for lettering became known, I was frequently asked to make signs for different clubs. It was great fun. Through the years, I've owned lots of pens and tried lots of different kinds of paints and inks. I can say that I still get excited with the process of lettering and using all the different tools and materials that are available today.

FAVORITE WRITING INSTRUMENTS

The pointed pen is my favorite instrument for writing, which of course I use for Copperplate script, a cursive lettering style that I enjoy. An important suggestion I have for using nibs for the pointed pen is to rub new metal tips with a small cloth dipped in gum arabic. This will help remove the manufacturer's film off of the tips and help the ink and paint bind better to the metal.

FAVORITE LETTER

With its straight stem and curves, I think the letter "B" is a very nicely balanced letter. Because of this balance, and perhaps because I've practiced it a lot since it is the first letter of my name, it is my favorite.

Barb's Masking Fluid Letters

Masking fluid is one of the most exciting mediums to use for hand lettering. Couple that with a writing instrument created from a chopstick, and the excitement doubles. Maybe triples. There is a bit of imperfection to these letters, and that's the way they should be—imperfect, playful, and just plain old fun.

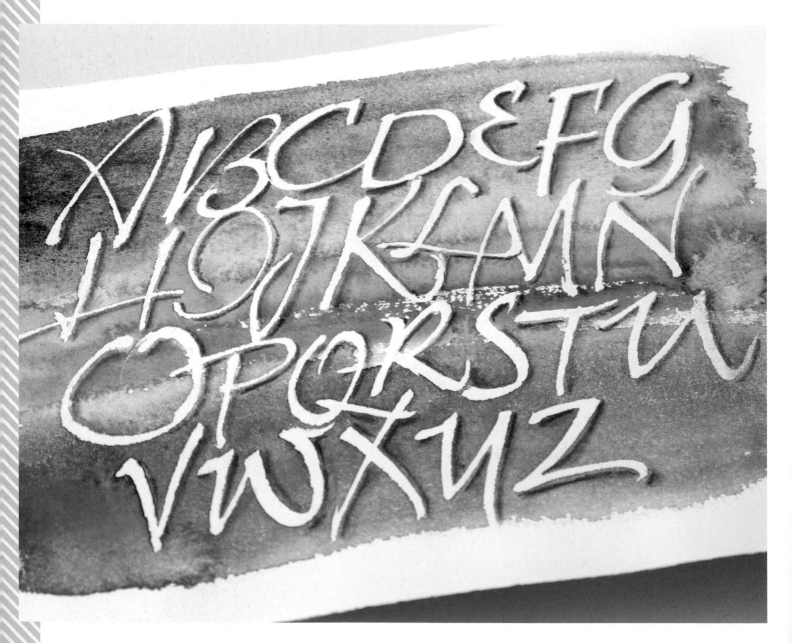

fig. A

fig. B

fig. C

WHAT YOU'LL NEED

* Chopstick
* Sharp blade or utility knife
* Pencil
* Scratch paper
* Masking fluid
* Small plastic container
* Watercolor paper
* Wide, flat paintbrushes
* Watercolors
* Rubber cement pickup

TECHNIQUE

1 Shave the tip of a wooden chopstick at a 45-degree angle on both sides, using a sharp blade. Smooth out any rough spots with the blade.

2 Imagine how you want your letters to look. Practice the letters with a pencil and paper first.

3 Pour a small amount of masking fluid into a plastic container and dip the chopstick pen into the fluid, allowing about a ¼ inch (6 mm) of the tip to be immersed. Create the letters that you have imagined and practiced onto the watercolor paper with the chopstick pen and masking fluid. Let the fluid dry for approximately one hour **(fig. A)**.

4 Load a wide, flat paintbrush with a watercolor and stroke it onto the paper. Allow it to dry partially but not completely **(fig. B)**.

5 Moisten the next section, where you plan to add a second color, right next to the first color, using a clean paintbrush loaded just with water.

6 Load the wide flat paintbrush with a second color and add a stroke onto the paper, right next to the first color, allowing the colors to slightly blend **(fig. C)**.

7 Repeat steps 5 and 6 until the coloring is complete. Let the piece completely dry.

8 Peel off the masking fluid by gently rubbing the surface of the dry paper with the rubber cement pickup.

Textured Letters

The beauty of this project is that after you create the outline of the letter that you choose, you can let almost anything happen within the chunky space created by the outline. You can doodle, stamp, paint, collage, and more. The letterforms I use for this project are based on the versals hand. I like these letters because they have good, substantive stems. But other letterforms will also work. You just have to practice getting the form down, and then embellishing the inner part of the forms.

fig. A

fig. B

fig. C

fig. D

WHAT YOU'LL NEED

* No. 2 pencil
* Watercolor paper
* Black fine-tip marker
* Black sumi ink
* Small round brush
* Watercolors
* Paper stump (see page 80)
* Note: See Variations for other possible supplies

TECHNIQUE

1 Lightly sketch the form of a letter onto a piece of watercolor paper, using a No. 2 pencil.

2 Divide the stem into smaller segments with a fine-tip marker, and make assorted marks and doodles in the segments **(fig. A)**.

3 Outline the letter with black sumi ink, using the small round brush **(fig. B)**. Moisten small sections of the work with water, and add watercolors to the moistened sections. There is no need to allow each section to fully dry. Allow lights, mediums, and darks to work together and slightly blend into each other **(fig. C)**.

4 Create shadows by outlining the letter with pencil marks, then blend with a paper stump. When creating shadows, decide on where you want the shadows to fall. I like to create my shadows at the right and lower portion of the letter. Another option is to have the shading occur on the left and upper portions. Whichever option you choose, be consistent **(fig. D)**.

VARIATIONS

There are many other methods that you can use to decorate the letterforms. Here are some ideas:

* Use a small stencil and sponge to add patterns with inks and paints.
* Collage assorted papers by adhering them to the paper with a glue stick.
* Apply a small amount of gesso or adhesive; while it is still tacky, rub it with a small amount of foil.
* Add doodles with watercolor pencils, and blend them with water and a small round brush.
* Create small concentrated "bee stings" of color with an extra small round brush loaded with concentrated color.
* Add doodles and marks with gel and metallic pens.
* Paint a section and sprinkle on a small amount of metallic powders.
* Attach stickers.
* Outline a doodle with a graphite pencil and rub it with your finger to make it blend and smudge.
* Punch paper shapes and attach them with a glue stick.

barbara close 123

As much as I love lettering, I also love to paint. This is a canvas that I started by painting the background with blues, greens, and white. I used inks, paints, and markers to add assorted text. Aside from varying the tools and materials, I like to vary the direction of text on a piece: from left to right, right to left, bottom to top, diagonally, and in a slight curve.

LAURIE'S SHELL

Aside from the pointed pen, I really love to letter using a seashell that was given to me by artist Laurie Doctor. It's a shell with a long pointed end and I dip that end into whatever paints or inks that I'm using and letter with it. It's so unusual but because I have used it so much, it has become a pleasantly familiar lettering tool for me.

This alphabet is inspired by the brush stroke—a style that is loose, modern, and conceived by the marks that a brush would make, rather than what a metal nib would make. Using a brush or a found object instrument, such as a chopstick or a stick, would work well for this alphabet.

Rhianna Wurman

www.rhicreations.blogspot.com

You know you're a lettering artist when you collect magazine clippings of ads, flyers, and other materials just for the creative logos and lettering. I have boxes and drawers full of clippings and cards from here and there. When I started school for graphic design, it got even more intense. I started to catch myself looking at ads, movie titles, books, and building signs, and dissecting the type and letterforms used in them. I still practice this habit to this day, but it's a good habit to have as a lettering artist. It means you are paying attention and taking inspiration to expand your knowledge and creativity.

FAVORITE LETTER

The cursive "Y" is my favorite. Just saying the letter is fun. We say it all the time! It's a curious letter at heart. The bottom stroke of the Y, or the descender, can be so beautiful. I often add lots of curves to my last stroke. I especially love when a word ends in "Y" because I can extend the stroke to frame my words, if it fits nicely with the piece I'm working on.

FAVORITE WRITING INSTRUMENTS

My favorite lettering tools are Sakura Gelly Roll pens in white, Staedtler pigment liner pens, Sakura Pigma Micron pens in black, and mechanical pencils. A good old mechanical pencil is the basis for most of my lettering works, because it offers a very neat line and does not require constant sharpening.

Feathered Alphabet

This alphabet is all about freehand doodling. Once you feel comfortable doodling several motifs, such as feathers and leaves, the process becomes very organic as you allow yourself a free flow of movement to fill each letter shape. To complete an entire alphabet in this style takes a lot of patience. When I got stuck or tired, I took little breaks in between.

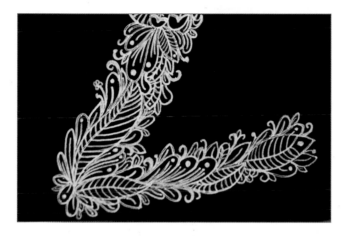

WHAT YOU'LL NEED

* Mechanical pencil (0.7mm)
* Scratch paper
* High-quality black paper
* White pen
* Scanner (optional)
* Computer with Photoshop software (optional)

TECHNIQUE

1 Practice doodling feathers, leaves, vines, flowers, and other desired motifs on scratch paper until you feel comfortable with several of the motifs. Also practice sketching simple block letter shapes.

2 Lightly sketch simple block letter shapes onto black paper, using a mechanical pencil.

3 Using a mechanical pencil, doodle feathers, leaves, vines, and flowers in various sizes and in a random fashion to fill the sketched letter shapes.

4 Trace over the pencil doodles with a white pen.

5 Trace over the white pen work a second time, to make the lines thicker. Let dry.

6 Erase any stray pencil marks.

7 This method can be used in lots of different types of art. To make a complete alphabet as shown here, you can opt to scan the letters on your computer using Photoshop.

8 Use Photoshop to clean up any stray marks, size the letters, arrange them, and to print.

TIP

Occasionally, I skip the pencil sketching and doodling and go straight into the work with a white pen. It sometimes feels more natural that way. Try both ways to see which you prefer.

Favorite Words

This piece is a collection of my favorite words. I lettered them with a mixture of block letters, serif and non-serif letters, script letters, and letters created with organic lines and doodles.

fig. A

fig. B

WHAT YOU'LL NEED

* Mechanical pencil (0.7mm)
* Fine-point ink pen or marker
* Vellum drawing paper
* Scanner (optional)
* Computer with Photoshop software (optional)

TECHNIQUE

1 Select a word and lightly create a cursive sketch of it onto the paper. Create a second stroke close to the first sketch, to uniformly thicken the letters so that they become a blocked cursive style **(fig. A)**.

2 Correct any of the marks with an eraser, and re-sketch certain parts as needed.

3 Create a third set of strokes on the left and lower portions of the word and add small lines. Erase any unwanted pencil marks **(fig. A)**.

4 Using a different word, repeat steps 1–2 and color in the blocked cursive word with the black marker pen. Erase any unwanted pencil marks.

5 Select other words in varying styles to letter onto the paper until the entire page is filled. Erase any unwanted pencil marks after each word **(fig. B)**.

6 Leave as is or opt to scan the piece onto your computer and use Photoshop to clean up any stray marks, add color, and print.

DOODLING & LETTERING

I am quite obsessed with doodling. I'm the girl who doodled during class when I should have been taking notes. Doodling is a creative release for me. So naturally, my lettering and doodling go hand-in-hand. To me, doodling and lettering work well together. It's visually interesting to see letters that are made up of various objects or unexpected lines.

This is a saying that my grandma always used. I tried to create whimsy with a mixture of upper and lowercase cursive and regular print letters, in both thick blocks and thin strokes.

MY STYLE

My style of lettering is whimsical with a vintage flair for good measure. It's never straight and perfect. I don't use a ruler to construct each letter. Instead, I let the letters flow from my hand and trust the movement. My lettering suits my style of quirky and playful illustrations. Because I have always been a lover of vintage ads and posters, I love the elegance in vintage lettering and have picked up a bit of that in my own works. My goal is to make people feel inspired and cheerful.

i'm me & i'm proud

I wanted to make a bold statement of self-confidence, something that I'm growing into. I've learned that every person is different, and it's good to be quirky. That's what makes us special. I made the letters large and in a block letter style, with contrasting black and white to pack a punch.

Martha Lever

www.marthalever.blogspot.com

I can remember as far back as first grade, writing on those lined papers with a chunky pencil. I remember being able to form the letters correctly and I think I became hooked then. As I grew, I just always loved to write. I also taught fourth grade and I loved writing on the chalkboard with the chalk. When I was about 30, I picked up a calligraphy nib, went to my first class, and fell completely in love with calligraphy. From that point on, I've been pursuing the art of calligraphic lettering.

FAVORITE WRITING INSTRUMENTS

I have many lettering tools that I absolutely love, but I think the tool I grab the most is a plain old No. 2 pencil. I love to draw letters with a pencil and shade the letters, or just work out a layout for a quote. The humble pencil helps me do all of this without too much fanfare.

FAVORITE LETTER

I love a capital "A" in my Chunky Versal style, but I struggle with the capital "A" in a calligraphic italic. So it depends on the lettering style that I am using, as to which letters I favor.

Decorated Versal Framed Letters

These letters are made by first creating a modern and chunky letter based on the medieval versal style of writing. Historically, the versal hand was used to begin a verse or chapter in hand-lettered medieval documents. After that, it's all about framing, doodling, and coloring so that the letter comes to life. The main tip to keep in mind with these letters is to know when to stop. Sometimes, going overboard with the doodling can make the overall letter look too busy and hard to enjoy.

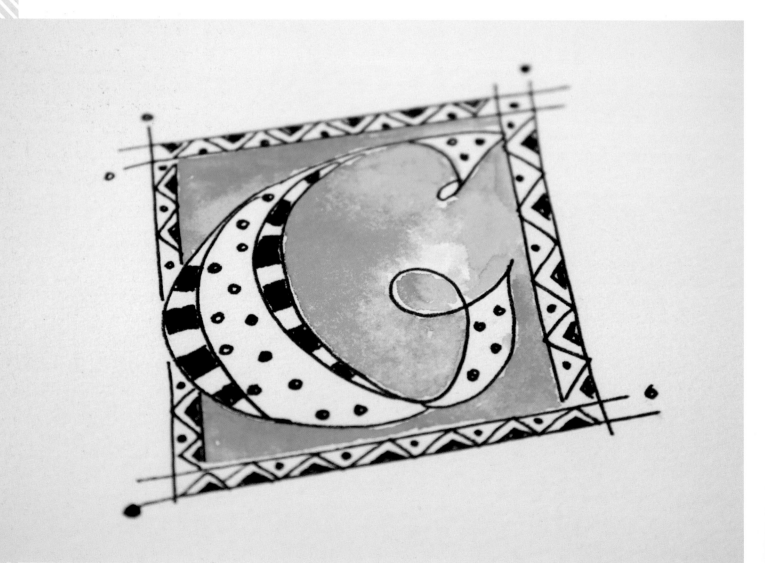

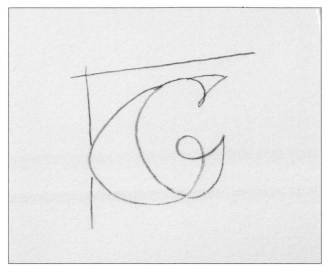

fig. A

fig. B

fig. C

WHAT YOU'LL NEED

* Pencil
* Hot-press watercolor paper
* Fine-point monoline marker, black
* Watercolors
* Paintbrush

TECHNIQUE

1 Draw a chunky versal letter on watercolor paper with a pencil **(fig. A)**.

2 Draw a box around the letter and create a double line for a frame.

3 Outline the letter and box with a black marker **(fig. B)**.

4 Add doodles in the frame and within the letter with a black marker.

5 Paint the letter and box with coordinating watercolors **(fig. C)**.

6 Add more doodles to complete.

SEASONS OF LETTERING

In earlier seasons of my life, when I started on the road to becoming a lettering artist, I stayed strictly within the classical letterforms. These included Italic, Roman, Foundational, and Uncial, to name a few. Years later, with much experience under my belt, I am in a new season of my artistic lettering life. Now my lettering is colorful, whimsical, and experimental. I love drawing these chunky versals for titles and for quotes in my journals and finished pieces.

Katie

Once you get the hang of lettering the chunky versal, you'll be able to make this project in no time. It's an ideal one for lettering a child's name and hanging the finished piece on their door or in their baby book or scrapbook. The piece can also be framed.

fig. A

fig. B

fig. C

WHAT YOU'LL NEED

* Pencil
* Hot-press watercolor paper
* Die cutter with frame motif (optional)
* Fine-point monoline marker, black
* Watercolors
* Paintbrush

TECHNIQUE

1 To create a frame motif, cut the paper in a die cutter. If you do not have a die cutter, you can cut a frame shape freehand, or use a rectangular piece of paper.

2 Using a pencil, letter a person's name in the chunky versal style.

3 Outline the name with a black marker (**fig. A**).

4 Add doodles within portions of letters with a black marker (**fig. B**).

5 Paint the letter with coordinating watercolors (**fig. C**).

6 Add more doodles to complete.

TRANSPARENCY TRICK

For me, the painting stage is usually intuitive but the lettering is completely planned out. One of my favorite tricks with composing lettered works is to use a transparency sheet as a test sheet that I use over my background to try out different layouts with a marker. The marker can be wiped off easily if I make a mistake.

Historically, versal letters can be seen as extremely ornate, typically used to create an initial character on a page or chapter. My alphabet is a modern interpretation of the versal hand, which I call the Chunky Versal. It is a hand with thick stems and playful serifs.

Here's a piece made by lettering the words with the Chunky Versals and then doodling small flowers within the space of each of the letters for "Flower." After that, the flowers were colored in with markers and then the negative space filled in with a black marker. A light gray marker was also used to outline the words, to create a shadow effect.

PRACTICE POSITIVE

There are many lettering artists out there whom I admire and whose lettering skills are far, far superior to mine; but I try to just admire and not covet. That will always be a constant struggle for me, but studying the work of others can be a positive thing. It makes me practice more to improve my skills, and practice is at the heart of becoming a better letterer. Practice, play, practice, doodle, practice, jump out of your comfort zone, practice some more, but most of all, have fun and keep evolving.

About the Contributors

ANDY AINGER has been creating hand drawn typography from an early age, with original inspiration from his dad's clean and consistent letters on workplace signs. Andy often uses traditional methods in conjunction with computer software to create his unique letters. To see more of his artwork, visit www.andyainger.com.

FRANÇOIS BÉGNEZ was practically born with a pen in his hand, and he was drawing comic book strips—focusing on the words in the title first—at a very young age. His favorite lettering tool is a felt-tip pen, and he often combines doodles with his letters. To see more of his work, visit www.francoisbegnez.com.

FLORA CHANG considers herself first a doodler and then a lettering artist. She's been doodling since an early age and once she started working as a greeting card designer, she started to integrate illustration with lettering for most of her works. She considers lettering as part of the illustration process. Learn more at www.happydoodleland.blogspot.com.

BARBARA CLOSE is a graphic designer and calligrapher from Southern California. She often combines her lettering with mixed-media for a fun, playful effect, always making sure to leave her margins white to add a sense of calm to her pieces. To learn more about her artwork, visit www.bcdezigns.com.

PHILIPPE DEBONGNIE was fascinated with logos at a young age, which has led to his lifelong love of lettering. He typically combines drawing with lettering, feeling like even a single word placed strategically in his artwork adds instant depth and meaning. To see more of his artwork, visit www.philippedebongnie.be.

KARYN DENTEN begins every piece of artwork with a new, sharp No. 2 pencil and a clean piece of paper. With a graphic design background, she often then transfers her work to the computer to add color and detail. To learn more about her, visit www.den10studio.com.

AIMEE DOLICH is a Boston, Massachusetts-based calligrapher who discovered the rapidograph in a high school art class and has been experimenting with lettering ever since. She always letters in black, adding color to enhance her work. To learn more, visit www.artsyville.blogspot.com.

LISA ENGELBRECHT is a Laguna Beach, California-based artist who loves to work on fabric because of its forgiving nature. She teaches lettering classes and workshops all over the world, sharing her knowledge of experimental lettering and the creative process. To learn more about her, visit www.lisaengelbrecht.com.

PAM GARRISON is a Southern California-based mixed-media artist. She received a calligraphy kit as a child and has been fascinated with pens, papers, and letters ever since. For Pam, there is no substitute for the art of hand lettering. To see more about her artwork, visit www.pamgarrison.com.

STINE KAASA is a designer and illustrator from Oslo, Norway. She designs her letters much like she designs her illustrations, which often leads to seamlessly combining the two in her artwork. To learn more about her, visit www.stinekaasa.org.

MARTHA LEVER is a calligrapher and mixed-media artist from Jacksonville, Florida. She fell in love with the art of calligraphy at the first touch of a calligraphy nib, and she often uses stenciling as background for her lettering. Visit www.marthalever.blogspot.com.

LINDA SCHNEIDER is a watercolor artist and calligrapher from Liberty Lake, Washington. Partial to a traditional style of lettering, she creates every piece not only with materials, but also with heart and emotion. To see more of her artwork, visit www.lindaschneiderart.com.

JESSICA SWIFT is a Portland, Oregon-based designer who creates with vibrant colors in her quest to make people happy through her art. She uses fun and quirky patterns and illustrations in conjunction with her letters to share messages of joy and braveness. To learn more about her, visit www.jessicaswift.com.

MADELINE TOMPKINS is one half of the mother-daughter duo Tag Team Tompkins, in which her lettering art combines with her mother's beautiful cut paper illustrations. To learn more, visit www.tagteamtompkins.etsy.com.

LORI VLIEGEN colored with her mom before bed when she was a young girl, and she's been going to sleep dreaming of letters ever since. She often combines watercolor doodles and drawings with her lettering work. To learn more, visit www.elviestudio.blogspot.com.

RHIANNA WURMAN has been doodling since kindergarten, and she now can't practice lettering without doodling on the same page. With a whimsical, vintage style of lettering, Rhianna aims to achieve a playful look in her artwork. Visit www.rhicreations.blogspot.com.

Index

A

About the Author....................144
About the Contributors...........142
Ainger, Andy.......................58
Anatomy of a Letter 7

B

Basics.............................. 7
Bégnez, François...................36

C

Chang, Flora 10
Close, Barbara 118
Cold-Pressed Paper 8

D

Debongnie, Philippe..............108
Denten, Karyn 46
Dolich, Aimee 52

E

Engelbrecht, Lisa 100

F

Featured Fonts and Styles/Hands 8

G

Garrison, Pam......................28

H

Hot-Pressed Paper 8
How to Make a Soda Can Pen......107
How to Use a Paper Stump 80

K

Kaasa, Stine.......................90

L

Lever, Martha......................134

M

Materials and Supplies 8

R

Rough Paper 8

S

Schneider, Linda...................68
Serif and Sans Serif Defined........49
Swift, Jessica......................20

T

Tompkins, Madeline 82

V

Vliegen, Lori 74

W

Wurman, Rhianna 126

About the Author

Jenny Doh is founder of www.crescendoh.com and lover of art. She is author and packager of numerous books including *Journal It!*, *We Make Dolls*, *Hand in Hand*, and *Signature Styles*. She lives in Santa Ana, California.

Like lettering? Try it in a journal. Visual journaling is an exciting blend of book arts, writing, and collage. To help you find plenty of inspiration and ideas for your work, nineteen mixed-media artists present several pages from their visual journals along with their favorite signature techniques, tips, and creativity boosters.